THE *NEW* STANDARD AMERICAN BRIDGE UPDATED

By
Norma Sands

www.normasands.com

ROCKY MOUNTAIN BOOKS

Published by
Rocky Mountain Books
Post Office Box 100663
Denver, Colorado 80210

Dedicated To

LEE SANDS
He has been a bright light in my life since the day he was
born. I am proud of my son, not because of his many
accomplishments, but because of who he is.

BONNIE LEGREID
She is the personification of a sister who is also a friend.
There is something very special about having a person in
your life who is supportive always.

And Special Appreciation To

Ann Perry
Debbie Taylor
Jan Janitschke
Pat and Chuck Henke
Ella Margaret Cron
Ken Perry

For all the time you so freely gave and for your
continued support, I say:
Thank you, thank you, thank you.
You will never know how much you are appreciated.

And thank you, Mike Lawrence.

If you want to get something accomplished ask the busiest
person you know. Mike Lawrence is a world champion
bridge player and the most prolific bridge writer alive. He
has written books on almost every topic in bridge and has
long been my favorite bridge author. Everything he has
written is worth reading. For a list of all his books and
software available, and how to obtain them, see:

www.MichaelSLawrence.com

Thank you Mike for all you have taught me and for writing the Introduction to my book.

TABLE OF CONTENTS

Introduction

"I just finished reading a very friendly book on bridge. It reminded me of that time in my life when I discovered bridge. Bridge is a game that captivates you and holds your attention forever. But it is not something that comes to you in a flash. It is something that you have to work on and you have to work on it in the right way. I know from experience that when you learn something the right way it is like taking three steps forward. If you learn something the wrong way, it is like taking one step forward and two steps backwards. In other words, you really want to get it right the first time.

This is where Norma's new book comes in. Her book gets it right and anyone reading it will know that they are going in the right direction.

For me, the marks of a good book on bridge are that it is readable, that it is accurate, and that it is useable. I am comfortable that this book includes all of these qualities. As a bonus, it goes further than it has to by showing the reader a hint of the special bidding methods that await after they have mastered the basics. ...students will be pleased, Norma."

Mike Lawrence

FOREWORD

Bridge fascinates, amuses and challenges millions of players on every level. When I think of the excitement I felt when first learning this game, I envy you. I still love the game, but the early stages are like falling in love for the first time. Learning bridge well requires effort, but it will be well worth the time spent; it will open up a new world for you by creating a bond with the millions of people who have learned to love the game. You will find bridge played from foursomes at home, to social parlor games, to international tournaments. If you have played a little and know the mechanics, move on to Chapter One; if not, don't skip anything.

The game of bridge consists of a series of hands in which the entire deck of 52 cards is dealt in clockwise rotation to the four players. Each hand consists of two phases, bidding and play. The bidding phase of the hand is frequently referred to as the auction since each bid is higher than the preceding bid until someone "buys" the contract. You bid to describe your hand, listen to what partner bids, and communicate information about your hands to know how much you should bid and whether you want to name a certain suit as trump or play without a trump suit. Your partner is the cheerful person across the table from you. After the bidding is complete, the hand is played. The object is to take at least as many tricks as you have bid or "contracted" to take. A trick is completed when a card is played from each hand in clockwise rotation. The person who plays the highest card of the suit led wins the trick, unless a trump is played.

The normal order of high cards exists. The ace is the highest, then the K, Q, J, 10, etc. You must play a card of the suit that is led if you have one, but when there is a trump suit and you have no cards of the suit led, you can capture the trick by playing a trump. For example, if an opponent led the ace of clubs and each hand followed suit with a club, the opponents would win that trick because the ace is always the highest. If, however, you were out of clubs, and hearts were trump, you could capture the trick by playing any heart. If more than one hand plays a trump, the highest trump would capture the trick. The fact that there is a trump suit does not mean that you have to trump if you are out of the suit led; you also have the option of discarding an unwanted card of another suit.

There are 13 possible tricks to be taken, since each person is dealt 13 cards. Whichever side takes more than six tricks has taken more than half. For bidding purposes, the number you bid is the number of tricks you hope to take *over six*. The first six tricks taken are referred to as your "book." If a pair has bid to 2♠, spades will be trump and eight or more tricks need to be taken to fulfill the bid (6 + 2). A bid of 3◊ means that diamonds will be trump and nine or more tricks are needed to make the contract. A bid of 1 Notrump (1NT) means that there is no trump suit and at least seven tricks are needed. A bid of six would mean twelve tricks need to be taken. This is all but one trick and is called a small slam. A bid of seven, contracting to take all the tricks, is called a grand slam. You get points if you make your contract, but if you fail to take as many tricks as you bid, the opponents will receive penalty points.

One thing that is different about bridge from most other card games is that there is a rank of the suits for bidding purposes. Clubs is the lowest- ranking, then diamonds, hearts, and spades. Notice that they are in alphabetical order. Clubs and diamonds are referred to as the minor suits, and hearts and spades as the major suits. Notrump (the absence of a trump suit) is higher-ranking than any suit. In bidding, each bid must be higher than the one preceding it. A bid of 1◊ would be higher than 1♣; a bid of 1♠ would be higher than 1♣, 1◊, or 1♡. If someone opened the bidding 1◊, anyone at the table could still bid 1♡ or 1♠ or 1NT (notrump), but if someone wanted to bid clubs, they would need to bid at least 2♣, since clubs are lower-ranking than diamonds. Over a 1♠ opener, someone could still bid 1NT, but any suit bids would have to be at least on the two level. If 1NT has been bid, all the one-level bids have been used up. This continues at each level all the way up through the seven level. 7NT is the highest bid that can be made.

The dealer begins the bidding with a pass or with a bid of a suit or notrump. If he thinks his hand is good, he will usually bid something. He can bid anything from one to seven of any suit or notrump. The vast majority of hands, however, are opened on the one level. The idea is to hope partner can bid also, and together to arrive at the best contract.

After the bidding has begun, it proceeds in clockwise rotation, each person having a turn to bid or pass. Once someone has opened the bidding, it continues until there are three consecutive passes. If a person passes at his first turn, he can still bid at a later turn. The last bid determines the final con-

Chapter ONE
BEGINNING BRIDGE

You are about to partake in a wonderful adventure. After the dealer has dealt all 52 cards, pick up your hand and sort it into suits, alternating colors: red, black, red, black. The reason for this is that it's very easy for your eyes to play tricks on you by doing something like putting a diamond in with your hearts and not notice it. You would be amazed how often this happens even to very experienced players. If you sort your cards with the same colors next to each other—spades and clubs together, or hearts and diamonds together—you are even more likely to make an error of this sort.

When you have learned the first 10-12 chapters you should be able to play comfortably with any qualified player anywhere. The higher-numbered chapters should take the reader to another level of bidding knowledge.

Point-count bidding assigns value to those cards most likely to take tricks. Aces are given 4 points, kings 3 points, queens 2 points, and jacks 1 point. These cards are called honors or high cards. The 10 is considered an honor also, but isn't big enough to be assigned any points. When you total up the points in your hand the total is called high card points: HCP. The acronym HCP is used almost always in bridge books or articles on bridge. The HCP in each suit adds up to 10 and there are four suits, so there are a total of 40 HCP in the deck. A hand with 10 HCP would be an average hand.

A	=	4 points
K	=	3 points
Q	=	2 points
J	=	1 point
10	=	---

13 is the number that has been used for many years as the amount of points needed to open the bidding with one of a suit.

Once your hand is sorted count your HCP. The dealer is the first person to speak by making a bid or passing. Basically, we open all hands with 13 or more HCP, and with 12 HCP we tend to open with any excuse.

You are dealt

♠ A Q J 7 5
♥ K 8 6
♦ 9 7
♣ K 9 3

The dealer on your right passed and it is your turn. You have 13 HCP and a long suit (five or more). With this hand you happily bid 1♠.

In the '50s and for several decades after, due to the strong influence of Goren and his prolific bridge writing, a singleton was fairly routinely given a value of 2 points even as opener. (There are still people who do this.) Because short suits become very valuable after a trump suit has been picked, the trend now is to count them after you know what suit is trump. A singleton may be a perk, but counting 2 points at the start may cause you to open some hands that are too weak. **Count HCP and consider other factors, perks* or flaws, with borderline hands.**

Again, we open hands with 13 HCP and open with 12 HCP if there is any excuse. With the above hand if the J of spades were the 9, we would have only 12 HCP. We would open that hand anyway, because our excuse is we have a good 5-card suit—"a perk." The short discussion of opening with one of a suit is to give you some awareness of opening bids at the one level. Opening with one of a suit is covered in detail in Chapter 2.

In this chapter the focus is on opening bids of 1NT and responding to it.

> OPEN WITH 1NT IF YOUR HAND CONTAINS
> EXACTLY 15, 16, 17, OR 18 HCP, AND IS BALANCED.

A balanced hand means no singletons or voids and no more than one doubleton. Below are two typical examples of opening 1NT hands:

♠ K 10 9   ♠ 6 2
♥ A J 6 5   ♥ A Q 8
♦ K Q 7 2   ♦ K Q 7 5 3
♣ K 2   ♣ A Q 7

* See *Page of Perks* after Chapter 6.

A brief discussion of scoring is necessary for you to understand the objectives in bidding. The amount of points you receive for making your contract varies depending on what was named as trump. Clubs and diamonds, the minor suits, are worth 20 points for each number you bid and make. For example, a bid of 2♣ would be worth 40 points (2x20), **if you take eight tricks** (six plus the number bid). Hearts and spades, the major suits, are worth 30 points for each number you bid and make. A bid of 3♡ means that hearts are trump, and if you take nine tricks, you would get 90 points (3 x 30). Notrump bids work a little differently. The first trick in NT is worth 40 points and all subsequent tricks are worth 30 points. A bid of 2NT making two, eight tricks in all, would be worth 70 points. A bid of 3NT making three, nine tricks, would be worth 100 points.

♣	20 points per trick bid and made	
♢	20 points per trick bid and made	
♡	30 points per trick bid and made	
♠	30 points per trick bid and made	
Notrump:	40 points for the first trick,	
	30 points for each subsequent trick	

One of the main objectives in bidding is to bid a game if your hand plus partner's is good enough. Games are important to bid because large bonus points are added to your score, later, for games bid and made. Bidding game means making a bid that would give you 100 points, or more.

Games: **Tricks needed**

4♡ or 4♠	=	Game	4 x 30 = 120	10
3NT	=	Game	40 +30 + 30 = 100	9
5♣ or 5♢	=	Game	5 x 20 = 100	11

Examples of Scores

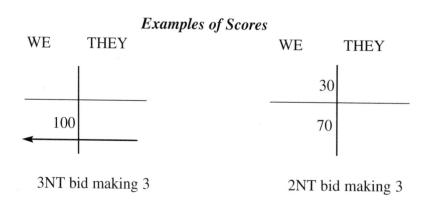

3NT bid making 3   2NT bid making 3

The line (with the arrow) indicates a game has been made. You will notice that in the first example a game has been bid and made. In the second example you also made 3, but because you only bid 2NT, you do not get credit for the game. The extra trick you took is counted, but you didn't win a game. The scores below the line record games or part scores and above the line record extra tricks, bonuses, and penalties incurred by the opponents. See the section on scoring at the end of this book—**notice the alternative method.**

You may wonder at this point how you can ever know if the combined hands are good enough for game. A guideline is that if it can be determined through the bidding that the two hands contain a total of 26 points, game should be bid, as **26 points will normally produce game in NT or a major suit.** A bit more may be needed if a minor suit is selected as trump, because you need 11 tricks. For future reference, a bid of 6 is a small slam and a bid of 7 is a grand slam; 33 points will usually produce a small slam, and 37 points, a grand slam.

Let's look at an example where you could know that your partnership has enough points for game. Your partner has opened 1NT and you have

♠ A 6 5
♥ 6 5
♦ A 7 6 5
♣ K 8 7 6

Your partner has announced 15-18 HCP, and you have 11 HCP. There is a total of 26+ points between the two hands. *You* know that there are enough points for game, so you should bid 3NT.

When partner has opened 1NT, if you are *willing* to play in a NT contract, with	
0-7	HCP, pass, as the partnership cannot have enough points for game.
8-9	HCP, bid 2NT. This invites partner to bid game (3NT) if he has the top of his bid (17 or 18 points).
10-14	HCP, bid 3NT. True, if partner has only 15, you may be on 25 points, but when you know you are, at *worst*, within one point of game, that's close enough.

PRACTICE HAND

North

♠ A 4 3
♥ K 6 4
♦ 8 7 6 5
♣ K 5 4

West

♠ Q J 2
♥ Q 10 7 3 2
♦ A 3 2
♣ 3 2

East

♠ 10 9 8 7
♥ J 9 8
♦ 9 4
♣ Q J 10 9

South (You)

♠ K 6 5
♥ A 5
♦ K Q J 10
♣ A 8 7 6

THE AUCTION
You

South	**West**	**North**	**East**
1NT	Pass	3NT	Pass
Pass	Pass		

Opening lead: 3 of ♡
Leading the 4th best card from the longest suit is the most common lead against a NT contract.

You (South) are declarer because you were the first to bid NT. Your LHO (left-hand opponent) leads the ♡3. Partner's hand (North) is the dummy so is spread faceup on the table. Looking at the two hands, you will see that you have two top winners in spades, the A and K; two top hearts, the A and K; and the same in clubs. This makes 6 tricks you can take anytime, but you need 9 tricks to make 3NT.

The diamond suit will produce 3 tricks if you are willing to lose a trick to the ace. You can win the opening lead in either dummy or your hand. With this hand it makes no difference so suppose you win the trick with the ♡K in dummy. You must always lead from the hand that took the trick, which in this case is dummy. Develop your diamonds immediately by playing a low diamond from dummy, and after East plays low, play the K from your hand. If, for reasons known only to him, West doesn't take his ace, keep playing diamonds. Take your 3 diamonds and the rest of your aces and kings and you are home free! You have bid and made a game.

QUIZ

1. Always open the bidding with one of a suit when you have ___ points.
2. To open the bidding with 1 NT, you need ___, ___, ___, or ___ HCP.
3. A bid of two means you have to take ___ tricks.
4. A bid of six is called a ___ ___ and you need to take ___ tricks.
5. The most you can bid in bridge is ___.
6. There are ___ HCP in a full deck.
7. An ace is ___ points, a king ___, a queen ___, and a jack is ___ point.
8. Game means getting at least ___ points below the line.
9. A bid of ___ in a minor suit will produce a game if the required number of tricks are taken.
10. A bid of ___ hearts or spades will produce a game if the required number of tricks are taken.
11. A bid of ___ NT will produce a game if the required number of tricks are taken.
12. If a partnership owns a total of ___ points, a game should be bid because it's likely to be made.
13. A bid of 3♠ making four is ___ points below the line and ___ points above the line.
14. A bid of 1NT making one is ___ points.
15. A bid of 4◇ making four is ___ points.
16. In scoring, the points for extra tricks, bonuses and opponents' penalties go ___ the line. Game points are written ___ the line.

ANSWERS

1. 13
2. 15, 16, 17, 18
3. 8
4. Small slam, 12
5. 7
6. 40
7. 4, 3, 2, 1
8. 100

9. 5
10. 4
11. 3
12. 26
13. 90, 30
14. 40
15. 80
16. Above, Below

Chapter TWO
OPENING BIDS

You may open the bidding at any level from one to seven. The vast majority of hands that you open will be one of a suit or 1NT. This gives your partner an opportunity to tell you about his hand. Often there are several bids taken before there is enough information passed to know what, if anything, should be trump, and if you should stop at a low level, bid a game or even a slam. It may become clear that there aren't enough points to bid a game or slam so you will play at some low-level contract and attempt to get a part of a game, which is called a part score or a partial. You may have an opportunity to complete your game on the next hand. As a note of reminder, in bridge the order of suits is ♣ ◇ ♡ ♠ & NT. The spade suit is the highest-ranking suit for bidding purposes, but notrump is higher than any suit.

We have already learned about an opening bid of 1NT. Opening bids of one of a suit are made on a great variety of hands. The point count for opening one of a suit is 13 to about 21 points (occasionally 22). Hands in excess of this are opened on the two level. In suit bidding we count our HCP, and on borderline hands, refer to the Page of Perks after chapter 6.

All hands with 13 HCP should be opened and hands with 12 HCP should be opened with any excuse or if there are no flaws. Hands with 11 HCP should rarely be opened. You need some type of good excuse such as a strong six-card suit, preferably a major.

In a nutshell:
Open all hands with 13 HCP and most hands with 12 HCP.

After determining if you have enough strength to open the bidding, the next decision is which suit to bid. If the hand contains one long suit (five cards or more), the decision is easy. Unless you have an opening NT hand, you simply bid one of your long suits, even if you have a shorter suit that is stronger. In attempting to determine if the hand should be played with a trump suit, length is what is important. If a hand is played with a particular suit as trump, the partnership should hold at least eight cards of the suit. When you and your partner have eight cards of a particular suit, obviously the opponents have only five, which gives you a considerable advantage. If you and partner hold a spade suit and a heart suit as listed below

YOU					PARTNER			
♠	A	K	Q	J	♠	9	8	7
♥	9	8	7	6	5	♥	10	4	3	2

hearts (not spades) should most definitely be the trump suit. The partnership has nine hearts and only seven spades. *LENGTH* is the primary consideration. The high heart honors, which are in the opponents' hands, will be losers for us regardless of which suit (or NT) is selected as trump. The advantage of hearts being trump is after you have played two rounds of trumps, the opponents may be out of trumps, and if it takes one more round of pulling trump, three rounds in all to finish the job, the opponents will be fresh out and you will have two left in your hand and one left in dummy. These are like aces in the hole.

For quite some years, the style of bidding five-card majors has been so widely used it is considered standard. It means that the opening bidder must have at least five hearts or five spades in order to open with 1♡ or 1♠.

If you are lucky enough to have two five-card suits, always open the higher-ranking suit first, regardless of quality. Suppose you have five spades and five hearts; begin with 1♠. If partner doesn't raise that suit you will next bid 2♡. If he hasn't raised either of your suits by now, for you to complete your story, bid your hearts again. Anytime in bridge if you bid a suit and partner doesn't raise the suit, you must have at least five cards to bid that suit again. We never rebid a four-card suit that partner hasn't raised. So if you open 1♠ and follow that with bidding hearts twice, you show no fewer than five spades and five hearts. The reason for not starting with hearts first and then bidding spades is that the latter auction consumes more bidding space and is therefore less efficient. This can be a very important factor in not getting too high too fast.

A hand that is good enough to open and does not have five or more hearts or five or more spades, no five-card minor, and is not suitable for a 1NT opening, is opened with the *longer* of the two minor suits. If your minor suits are the same length, such as four clubs and four diamonds, 1◊ is the recommended opening bid.

Opening the bidding with one of a minor is the only occasion in bridge when it's acceptable to open with a three-card suit. An example of this would be if you had, say, three spades, four hearts, three diamonds, and three clubs. The recommended bid is 1♣. To recap:

- With four diamonds and four clubs, 1◇ is the recommended opening bid. (This is assuming there is no obvious opening bid such as 1NT.)
- With three clubs and three diamonds, open with 1♣.

Most of these hands are balanced so it is likely that the point count is not 15-18 HCP or you would open 1NT in the first place.

Although it is possible to open a minor suit on a three-card suit, people tend to get an exaggerated notion as to the frequency of this happening.

WHEN YOU OPEN ONE OF A MINOR SUIT YOU WILL HAVE FOUR OR MORE CARDS IN THE SUIT WELL OVER 80% OF THE TIME.*

IF PARTNER OPENS 1♣ IT IS MORE ACCURATE TO PICTURE HIM WITH FOUR CARDS IN THE SUIT, AS THAT IS DECIDED-LY MORE LIKELY THAN THREE CARDS. STATISTICS SHOW THAT HE WILL HAVE FIVE CLUBS MORE OFTEN THAN THREE. AND NOW THE SHOCKER: **SIX** CARDS IN THE SUIT IS ABOUT AS LIKELY AS THREE CARDS, WITH SIX CARDS TAKING A SLIGHT LEAD.

For years people have referred to a 1♣ opening bid as a "short club." This statistical information makes the word "short" to be a very poorly chosen adjective. There is no real reason to assign a name to a minor suit opening.

- In bridge, short suits are: singletons, doubletons, or voids.
- Average-length suits are three or four cards.
- Long suits are five or more cards.

Years ago when some group felt compelled to assign a name to a 1♣ opener, it would have made more sense to call a 1♣ opener an average club. It would have caused much less confusion and misconceptions about minor-suit openers.

*When opening 1♣, 5 out of 6 times you will have four or more cards. When opening 1◇, the percentage of having four+ cards is in the high 90's.

In addition to the point-count guidelines we have already learned, deductions need to be made for "unguarded" honors. The reason for this is, for example, a singleton King is a "goner" if the ace of that suit is led. It is still better than a small card, however, as partner could have the ace or the queen. If you have an unguarded honor of a K, Q, or J, deduct one point. If you hold a singleton or doubleton in a suit, your point count would be as follows:

A = 4   The ace needs no guard.
K = 2
Q = 1
J = 0
K2 = 3   One card is a sufficient guard for a king.
Q6 = 1
J5 = 0

The above is only an approximation, not intended to be an exact answer to the value of these honors, but it is somewhat of an improvement. The table above is not perfect so don't worry if you don't completely understand it.

You are the dealer and you have the following hands. Practice counting your points and determining your opening bid.

1. ♠ A K 7 6
   ♥ Q 8 7
   ♦ 10 8 7 2
   ♣ A 5

2. ♠ 10 7 6 5 4
   ♥ A K 5 3
   ♦ A Q 4
   ♣ 7

3. ♠ A K 8 7
   ♥ A 8 7
   ♦ A 9 3
   ♣ Q 4 3

4. ♠ A Q 8 7 6
   ♥ Q 8 7
   ♦ 9 5 3
   ♣ Q 8

5. ♠ 7 6 4
   ♥ A 8 4 2
   ♦ A 7 6
   ♣ A Q 7

6. ♠ Q 8 7 6 2
   ♥ A J 8 7 6
   ♦ A 8
   ♣ A

7. ♠ A 8
   ♥ 9 5 3
   ♦ K Q 7 3
   ♣ K Q 9 8

8. ♠ Q 6
   ♥ K J 10 5 4
   ♦ A K 4 2
   ♣ 8 7

1. You have 13 HCP. Open 1◇, your longer minor.
2. Your point count is 13 HCP. You have a five-card suit; bid it. 1♠.
3. Open with 1NT. This hand has 17 HCP and is balanced.
4. Pass. Not strong enough.
5. You have 14 HCP, but no five-card major. Open 1♣.
6. You have 15 HCP. Open 1♠. With two five-card suits, open the higher-ranking regardless of quality.
7. You have 14 HCP. With two four-card minors, bid 1◇.
8. Even if you take a point from the ♠Q, you still have 12 HCP. Bid 1♡.

PRACTICE HAND

Practice this hand by laying out all four hands. The dealer is the first to begin the bidding.

North
♠ A Q 2
♥ 7 6 5
♦ 7 6 5 4
♣ A 4 3

West
♠ K 9 4
♥ 10 4 2
♦ 10 2
♣ Q 10 8 7 6

East
♠ J 7 5
♥ K Q J 9
♦ J 9 8
♣ J 9 2

South - Declarer
♠ 10 8 6 3
♥ A 8 3
♦ A K Q 3
♣ K 5

THE AUCTION
Dealer

East	South	West	North
	1NT	Pass	3NT
Pass	Pass	Pass	

South is the declarer and West is on lead. A standard lead in NT is fourth down from your longest suit, which is the ♣7. Count your top tricks, meaning tricks that you can take anytime you want without losing the lead. There are seven—one spade, one heart, three diamonds, and two clubs. You need nine tricks to make your contract. There are usually possible tricks to be found in addition to the top tricks. In this hand, the diamond suit has a total of eight cards. The opponents have only five. If those cards are three in one hand and two in the other, which is most likely, the last small diamond will be a winner, so you are up to an expected eight tricks. If this all works, you still need one more trick. In the spade suit, if you lead from your hand towards the AQ, and West plays low, play the Q. This is called a finesse. You will win the trick if West has the K and didn't play it. If, instead, West plays his K, it's easy. Win the A and your Q is good. Since you know that you need to play a spade toward the AQ for a finesse, win the club lead in your hand and do it now. If the K is located where you want it to be, you are likely to make your contract. It is important to start developing your possible tricks early.

QUIZ

1. If you have ____ or more HCP, you should open the bidding with one of a suit.
2. An opening bid of one heart or one spade shows no less than ____ cards in that suit.
3. A balanced hand of 15, 16, 17 or 18 HCP is opened with ____ .
4. ____ is the highest-ranking suit.
5. The minor suits are ____ and ____ .
6. The major suits are ____ and ____ .

YES OR NO:

7. It is acceptable to open the bidding with 1♣ or 1◊ on a three-card suit ____ .
8. It is acceptable to open the bidding with 1♣ or 1◊ on a two-card suit ____ .
9. If someone at the table has bid 1♡ and you want to bid your diamond suit, you must bid at least 2◊. ____

You are the dealer. What do you bid with each of the following hands:

10. ♠ A Q 2   11. ♠ J 8 4 3 2   12. ♠ 7 6 5 4 3
    ♥ 7 5   ♥ A 9 8 6 4   ♥ A K 6 3
    ♦ A 7 6 4   ♦ A K   ♦ A 9 2
    ♣ A K 4 3   ♣ 2   ♣ A

ANSWERS

1.	13	7.	Yes
2.	5	8.	No, no, a thousand times no.
3.	1NT	9.	Yes
4.	Spades	10.	1NT. 17 HCP and balanced.
5.	Clubs and Diamonds	11.	1♠. No second choice.
6.	Hearts and Spades	12.	1♠

Chapter THREE
RAISING PARTNER'S SUIT
(For the Teachers Who Use Limit Raises See Chapter 17)

Your choices of responses to your partner's opening bid of one of a suit are basically raising his suit, bidding a suit of your own, or bidding NT. **Anytime your hand contains 6 or more points, you should find some response, as partner's hand could be big enough for game opposite your six points.** With less than 6 points, you should pass.

Raise your partner's MAJOR suit with three or more cards in that suit. For example, raise 1♠ to 2♠ with 6-10 points even if you have three small spades. Since he has at least five when he opens a major, when you have three or more, the partnership has at least eight, which is enough for a trump suit.

At your first response you should have five or more cards of partner's minor to raise it. Although partner will usually have more than a three- card suit, minors produce the lowest scores so become our last choice.

If you decide to raise partner's suit, your point count determines how high to raise. Partner opens 1♡ or 1♠ and you have three-card support giving you eight trump.

When you discover this trump fit with partner DISTRIBUTION IS USEFUL SO BE SURE TO ADD IT IN TO YOUR POINT COUNT.

DOUBLETON	=	1 POINT
SINGLETON	=	2 POINTS
VOID	=	3 POINTS

If you are lucky enough to have four trump, making nine between you, promote your singleton and void.

SINGLETON NOW	=	3 POINTS
VOID NOW	=	5 POINTS

With a fourth trump the promotion to 3 and 5 points is not even a little bit of a stretch; in fact, apart from your short suits growing under these circumstances, the fourth trump (making nine for your side) is of value by itself. If partner's trumps happen to be AK543 and yours are 8762, about 40% of the time the suit will split 2-2 and you will have no trump losers; whereas you would always have to lose at least one with AK543 opposite 862. There are numerous situations where a fourth trump might be valuable. Counting the fourth trump as a point (with nine between you) is quite reasonable.

Raising partner's suit from 1♡ to 2♡ shows 6-10 points including distribution. If partner opens 1♡, bid 2♡ with each of the following three hands:

1. ♠ A 8 7 2	2. ♠ 8 7 6	3. ♠ 2
♥ Q 6 5	♥ 8 7 2	♥ 9 8 3 2
♦ 9 8 5 4	♦ A J 7 6	♦ A 4 3 2
♣ 3 2	♣ A 8 4	♣ 6 5 3 2
(7 Points)	(9 Points)	(7 Points)
		The singleton = 3
		The 4th trump is a perk
		by itself.

Raising a minor suit requires more trumps. Partner opens 1◊. Raise to 2◊ with:

♠ 6 4 3	♠ 3 2
♥ 3	♥ 6 2
♦ A J 6 5 3	♦ J 9 6 4 2
♣ J 5 4 2	♣ A 7 5 2

Notice that there is no four-card or longer major suit to bid. That would be our first priority because major suits count more.

Raising partner's suit from one to three shows 13 to 16 points, including distribution, and is forcing at least to game. 26 points are needed for game and the bidding has shown a combined count of 26 or more. If partner opens 1♠, raise to 3♠ on the following two hands:

1. ♠ 9 8 6 2	2. ♠ K 4 3 2
♥ 4	♥ A 7 5
♦ A 8 7 2	♦ Q 7 2
♣ A K 8 2	♣ A 7 5

If you want to raise partner's suit but have a golden 10, 11 or a bad 12 points (11ish), you temporize by bidding a new suit first, then give an encouraging raise of partner's suit at your second bid, such as:

Opener	Responder		Opener	Responder
1♥	2♣	or	1♥	1♠
2♦	2♥		2♣	3♥

Notice in this first auction we know that partner has 10+ points when he bid 2♣, so no jump is needed to show about 11 points.	In this second auction, the 1♠ bid shows only 6+ points, so the jump to 3♡ is needed to show about 11 points.

There is another way of showing the hand that is too good for a 2♡ raise besides the one listed above. The other method, which is used mostly by tournament players, is listed in chapter 17. For now we will use the method described in this chapter.

Raising partner's suit directly to game shows a hand that is weak in terms of high cards, but is a super-fitting hand. It should contain five+ trumps, an outside singleton or void, and about 6 HCP, give or take a couple. For example, if partner opens 1♠, bid 4♠ with:

♠ K 9 8 6 2	With partner bidding 1♠,
♥ — — —	this hand becomes a
♦ Q 10 6 3	**MAGIC HAND**
♣ 8 6 3 2	

If 4♠ doesn't make, it will likely prevent the opponents from being able to find their heart game. This magic hand bid works very well with hearts also. This bid is never used in the minors. The jump from one to four is reserved for the MAGIC HAND AND IS USED IN MAJOR SUITS ONLY, AND IT IS ALWAYS THE RESPONDER WHO MAKES THE BID.

PRACTICE HAND

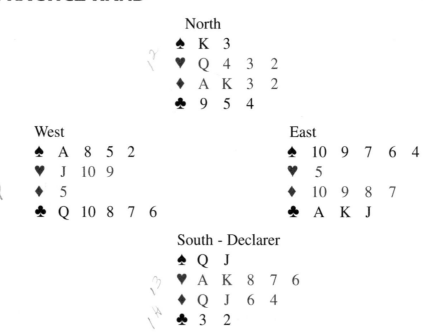

North
- ♠ K 3
- ♥ Q 4 3 2
- ♦ A K 3 2
- ♣ 9 5 4

West
- ♠ A 8 5 2
- ♥ J 10 9
- ♦ 5
- ♣ Q 10 8 7 6

East
- ♠ 10 9 7 6 4
- ♥ 5
- ♦ 10 9 8 7
- ♣ A K J

South - Declarer
- ♠ Q J
- ♥ A K 8 7 6
- ♦ Q J 6 4
- ♣ 3 2

South is declarer in a contract of 4♡. Opening lead: ◇5.

West is hoping partner can win the opening lead or some early trick and return a diamond, so he can trump it. Declarer, on this hand, must play trump immediately to remove all trump from the opponents' hands. Declarer will lose only the ace of spades and two club tricks, since he can trump any further club leads. He will lose three tricks and take the rest, making 4♡. If he fails to pull trump, he could get one of his diamonds trumped and lose too many tricks.

QUIZ

1. With ____ or more points, you should find some response to partner's opening bid of one of a suit.
2. You need to have _____ or more cards of partner's minor to raise at your first opportunity.
3. You need to have _____ or more cards of partner's major to raise at your first opportunity.
4. Raising partner's suit from 1 to 2 shows____ to____ points.
5. A singleton is worth____ points when raising partner's suit, and a void is worth ____ points when raising partner's suit.
6. A raise of partner's suit from 1 to 3 is____ (forcing or nonforcing).

Partner opens 1♡ and you have the following. What is your bid?

7. ♠ A 8 7 6 2   8. ♠ A Q 7 4   9. ♠ 7 6 4 3
   ♥ K 7 6   ♥ 7 6 5 2   ♥ A Q 5 4
   ♦ 8 7 2   ♦ A K   ♦ A Q 4 2
   ♣ 4 3   ♣ 10 9 3   ♣ 2

10. ♠ — ——   11. ♠ 8 7 4   12. ♠ 6 5 4
    ♥ K 8 7 6 2   ♥ A 6 5   ♥ 8 7 6
    ♦ Q J 6 2   ♦ 7 6 4 2   ♦ A Q 8 7 6
    ♣ 8 7 6 2   ♣ 7 6 2   ♣ 3 2

ANSWERS

1. 6
2. 5
3. 3
4. 6-10
5. 2 for singleton and 3 for void when you have 3 trump. Promote to 3 for singleton and 5 for a void if you have a 4th trump and partner has opened showing 5 (you have nine trump between you).
6. Forcing

7. 2♡
8. 3♡
9. 3♡
10. 4♡
11. Pass
12. 2♡

Chapter FOUR
RESPONDING TO ONE OF A SUIT
BY BIDDING A NEW SUIT
OR NOTRUMP

When you are considering bidding a suit of your own over partner's opening bid of one of a suit, pay the most attention to your HCP. Do not add value for shortness. You may count it later if you and partner agree on a trump suit. **Responding** *with a suit of your own on the one level such as (1♣—1♡) shows at least four cards of the suit you bid and 6-18 points,* possibly more. Notice that this is a very wide range. It is therefore forcing on partner to bid again, because if you happen to have a very big hand, you will want to bid a game, even possibly a slam.

In auctions involving suit bidding,

A NEW SUIT BY RESPONDER IS FORCING

Once again, a new suit at the one level shows at least six points and could be a very big hand. If partner opens one of a minor and you have any four-card or longer major suit, you should bid it, assuming you have at least six points. Don't be afraid to show a four-card major that is weak, even four small. Occasionally you may have a longer minor suit, which you choose to bid first. This would require bidding at the two level and then bidding again, so this auction should indicate a good hand.

If you have four hearts and four spades, respond with 1♡. If partner has four hearts, he will raise your hearts immediately. If not, he will bid a four-card spade suit if he has it. You will find out very early in the bidding if you have a major suit fit. **If you have five hearts and five spades, respond 1♠.** If partner doesn't raise your spades, you will next bid hearts. **Anytime in bridge when you have five hearts and five spades, you should bid spades first.**

However, if the bidding were to go

South	West	North	East
1◇	Pass	1♠	Pass
2◇	Pass	2♡	

responder has shown five spades and four hearts. With two five-card suits, he would have to bid **HEARTS AGAIN** to complete the picture of 5-5.

Responding with a suit of your own on the two level, called a two-over-one bid, shows a fairly good hand, or possibly a very good hand. It should describe a hand of 10 HCP, at a minimum, and four or more cards of the suit you bid. This occurs when the suit you want to bid is lower-ranking than the suit your partner opened. In these examples,

	Partner	You
1.	1♡	2♣
2.	1♠	2◇
3.	1◇	2♣

the new suit at the two level is, of course, forcing on partner to bid again because you have 10-18+ points.

Responding with a **deliberate** jump in a new suit (1◇—2♠, 1♡—3♣) is a super hand, 19 or more points. This jump shows a hand so big that game is guaranteed, and slam must be considered. The suit in which you are jumping should be at least five cards long.

■ The hand can contain fewer HCP if your suit is a good six+ card suit such as

♠ A K Q 10 4 3
♥ A K J 3
♦ 4 2
♣ 7

■ Also the HCP could be relaxed if you have a fit for partner's opening suit, such as partner opened 1◇ and you have a good five-card spade suit and also have four or more good diamonds.

Another frequently used response is 1NT. **A 1NT response shows a hand of 6-10 HCP, denies having a four-card or longer heart or spade suit that could be bid at the one level; and if partner has opened a heart or a spade, it denies holding three or more cards of his major suit.** The 1NT response does *not* even suggest a balanced hand.

When partner has opened one of a suit, a response of 2NT is made with a balanced hand of 13-15 HCP. A response of 3NT is made with a balanced hand of 16-18 HCP. These bids should not be in preference to bidding your four-card major suit, if you can do so on the one level. Suppose your partner opens 1♠. With 13+ points and a five-card minor you would bid it unless the suit is very weak, and you deny spade support so your hand would usually be 4-4-3-2, with the doubleton being in spades.

Plan your responses to the following bids, given the following hands. *Remember, with 6 points you should find something to bid.*

Partner opened 1◇
1. ♠ Q 8 6 2
   ♥ A 7
   ♦ 9 7 4
   ♣ J 8 6 3

Partner opened 1♣
2. ♠ 5 3 2
   ♥ A 6 4
   ♦ K 6 4
   ♣ J 9 7 3

Partner opened 1♠
3. ♠ 8 6
   ♥ 6 3
   ♦ A Q 8 6 3
   ♣ J 9 7 2

Partner opened 1♡
4. ♠ A 4
   ♥ 9 6 2
   ♦ J 8 6 2
   ♣ K 8 6 3

1. You should bid 1♠. Your partner could have four spades, so you could have a spade fit (eight or more cards between the two hands is enough to have a trump suit). If you respond with 1NT, you would be telling your partner that you don't have either four hearts or four spades.

2. Respond with 1NT. You do have four of partner's clubs, but as a first response, you should have five cards to raise partner's minor suit.

3. Bid 1NT. You would like to bid your diamond suit, but your hand isn't good enough. If partner had opened 1♣, you could bid 1◇, but partner opened 1♠. You need 10 HCP to bid a new suit of your own on the two level. The 1NT response often is useful as a "catch-all."

4. Raise to two hearts. This is *not* a two-over-one response. This is simply

raising partner's suit and it shows 6-10 points including distribution. You should raise partner's suit instead of bidding NT because partner shows at least five when opening with one heart or one spade. You make partner's job easy. He now knows that the hand will be played in hearts so all he has to do now is decide if the combined hands have enough points to be in game.

PRACTICE HAND

North
♠ A J 6 5
♥ A 2
♦ 9 8 7
♣ Q J 4 3

West
♠ Q 8 7
♥ 9 8 6 5
♦ A K Q
♣ 10 9 8

East
♠ 10 9
♥ Q J 10 7 4
♦ J 10 3 2
♣ 7 2

South
♠ K 4 3 2
♥ K 3
♦ 6 5 4
♣ A K 6 5

THE AUCTION

North	East	South	West
1♣	Pass	1♠	Pass
2♠	Pass	4♠	Pass
Pass	Pass		

AN OPENING HAND OPPOSITE AN OPENING HAND BELONGS IN GAME.

The opponents begin by taking the K, A, and Q of diamonds, followed by a heart which you win in your hand. You are now "booked," which means that you can't lose any more tricks and still make your contract. The only problem is a possible trump loser. You play the K and then lead towards your AJ6. If your left-hand opponent plays small, and he should, you play the J.

(If you don't do this and instead play the A at the second lead of trump, odds are against East having the lone trump Q at this point.) After winning the J, next play the A and all the trumps will be removed from the opponents' hands. The rest is easy.

QUIZ

1. Anytime you have ___ or more points, you should find some response when partner opens the bidding with one of a suit.
2. A two-over-one bid shows a minimum of ___ HCP.
3. A 1 NT response shows ___ - ___ HCP.
4. A jump shift shows ___ or more points.
5. If partner opens with 1♣ and you have enough points to bid, with five hearts and five spades, you should bid ___ first.
6. If partner opens with 1♣ and you have enough points to bid, with four hearts and four spades, you should bid ___.
7. A response of 2NT shows ___ to ___ HCP.
8. A response of 3NT shows ___ to ___ HCP.

Partner opens with 1♢. What is your first response with each of the following hands?

9. ♠ 9 8 7 5 3
   ♥ A K 7 6
   ♦ 8 7
   ♣ 6 5

10. ♠ A Q 7 6
    ♥ K 7 6 5
    ♦ 8 7
    ♣ 7 6 4

11. ♠ A 7 6 5 3
    ♥ A K 8 7 6
    ♦ K 4
    ♣ 2

12. ♠ A K 5 4 3
    ♥ A 2
    ♦ A 2
    ♣ K 7 6 5

13. ♠ 7 6 5
    ♥ 6 5
    ♦ 8 6 2
    ♣ A Q J 4 3

14. ♠ A 4 3
    ♥ K 6 5
    ♦ K 5 3
    ♣ A 10 7 5

15. ♠ 8 3
    ♥ Q 6 5 2
    ♦ Q 6 5 3
    ♣ K 5 3

ANSWERS

1. 6
2. 10
3. 6-10
4. 19
5. Spades
6. 1♡
7. 13-15
8. 16-18

9. 1♠
10. 1♡
11. 1♠
12. 2♠ 18 HCP and a couple of perks: rich in aces and kings & a good five-card suit.
13. 1NT
14. 2NT
15. 1♡

Chapter FIVE
SECOND BIDS—BY OPENER

Once the bidding has been opened and partner has responded, opener will clarify the size of his hand with his rebid. (Opener's second bid is usually called his rebid.) Sometimes you won't know, at this point, where the hand should be played, but other times it will be clear to you that a trump suit has been found (eight or more).

If you open   ♠   A   4   3   2
                          ♥   A   2
                          ♦   A   J   3   2
                          ♣   7   6   5

with 1◊ and partner responds 1♠, you should raise to 2♠. It's important to set the trump suit early. Partner must have at least four spades, so you know you have eight or more between you. A minimum opening hand is a hand of 13-15/16 points. You have a minimum hand so you raise a minimum level. REMEMBER THAT A PASS CANNOT BE CONSIDERED AS PART-NER'S HAND COULD BE BIG ENOUGH FOR GAME OR EVEN SLAM.

You open 1♡ with   ♠   A   2
                          ♥   A   J   5   4   3   2
                          ♦   K   3   2
                          ♣   4   3

and your partner responds 1♠; your rebid should be 2♡. Rebidding the suit shows a minimum opener, 13-15/16, and suggests more than a five-card suit.

If you open 1◊ with   ♠   A   2
                          ♥   K   9   3
                          ♦   K   Q   3   2
                          ♣   J   7   6   5

and partner responds 1♠, you should rebid 1NT. This shows a balanced hand that has fewer points than the opening NT range. It pinpoints your range to 12, 13, or 14 HCP. You could have bid 2♣, your other four-card suit, but 1NT is more descriptive. A rebid of 2◊ should not be considered; **an unsupported four-card suit is never rebid in bridge.**

Opener can jump a level of bidding to show bigger than minimum hands. If opener jumps to a new suit, called a **jump shift,** it shows 19+ points. There are different jumps available to opener. He can jump in his own suit, he can jump in partner's suit, he can jump in notrump, or as indicated above, he can jump in a new suit.

> **ANYTIME OPENER JUMPS AT HIS SECOND TURN, IT SHOWS A STRONG HAND.**

When rebidding, if you know where a hand should be played and you have enough points for game, <u>bid it.</u>

If you open 1♡ with   ♠   A   3
                        ♥   A   J   6   5   4
                        ♦   A   K   Q   5
                        ♣   8   7

and partner raises you to 2♡, bid 4♡. The trump suit has been set and partner has 6-10 points. Even if partner has only 6 points, with your 20 there are enough for game. **A trump suit has been found so distribution is counted.**

With some hands you will know that there are not enough points for game, so you will want to stop at a low level.

If you open 1♡ with   ♠   A   5
                        ♥   A   K   7   6   5
                        ♦   J   8   2
                        ♣   6   5   4

and partner raises you to 2♡, you should pass. Partner has 6-10 points and you have 13, so there are at best 23 points between the two hands. Unless you are hopeful of being in game, there is no point in bidding any higher.

With some hands, you may have enough points for game, but you can't be sure.

You open 1♠ with   ♠   A   J   8   6   4
                      ♥   A   K   5   4
                      ♦   K   5
                      ♣   3   2

and your partner raises you to 2♠. You have found a trump suit; your problem on this hand is to determine whether or not there are enough points for game. You have 17 points. If partner has 6-7, game should not be bid; but if partner has 9-10, you would want to be in game. Bid 3♠. This gives the decision to partner. If he has 6-7 points, he passes; with 9-10 he should accept your game invitation by bidding 4♠; and if he should happen to be in the middle of his range, 8 points, he will have to use his judgment.

PRACTICE HAND

```
                        North
                        ♠  K  5
                        ♥  A  Q  3  2
                        ♦  K  J  3  2
                        ♣  8  6  2
        West                              East
        ♠  A  9  8  7                     ♠  Q  J  10  6  2
        ♥  10  9                          ♥  K  8
        ♦  7  6                           ♦  10  5  4
        ♣  K  Q  J  7  5                  ♣  10  9  4
                        South
                        ♠  4  3
                        ♥  J  7  6  5  4
                        ♦  A  Q  9  8
                        ♣  A  3
```

THE AUCTION

South	West	North	East
		1♦	Pass
1♥	Pass	2♥	Pass
4♥	Pass	Pass	Pass

Notice the South hand bids game at the second turn, as the hand has 13 points with distribution.

West leads the ♣K. You win with the A and play a low heart. When your left-hand opponent plays low, you finesse the Q. Unfortunately, it loses to the K. Back comes a club, which is won by the J. The club Q is continued, which you trump in your hand. You now play another heart to your A, which picks up all of the outstanding trumps. How do you play the rest of the hand?

You have lost two tricks. You will need to come back to your hand with a diamond and play a low spade to your K, hoping the A is on your left. You can afford only one more loser. If LHO plays low, play your spade K.

SECOND BIDS—BY RESPONDER

When responder has bid a new suit at the one level, it shows at least four cards of the suit bid and 6-18 points. This is anything from a weak hand to a very good hand so responder's second bid must be carefully selected.

As responder, a minimum rebid of your own suit (if partner hasn't raised it) shows less than an opening hand and usually a six-card suit. The general rule is that if opener rebids NT, responder can rebid a five-card suit; but if opener rebids his own suit or changes suits, responder should have six cards to rebid his own suit.

If you have
- ♠ 7 6
- ♥ A Q J 4 3 2
- ♦ 6 5
- ♣ 4 3 2

and you responded 1♡ over partner's 1◇ opening, if partner rebids 2♣, you should rebid 2♡. Often with only 7 points you would pass at your second turn. However, your heart suit is good and you have little support for either of partner's suits.

At your second response a minimum raise of partner's suit or NT bids below the game level also show less than an opening hand.

If you have
- ♠ A 4
- ♥ A 6 5 4
- ♦ 6 5 4
- ♣ 8 6 4 2

and partner opened with 1◇, you would respond with 1♡. If partner next bid 1♠, you should bid 1NT. You don't want to pass as partner presumably has only four spades (with five he would have opened 1♠), and you have only two spades. Your 1 NT bid shows 6-10 HCP.

If partner opens 1♡ and you have

```
♠  A  6  5  4
♥  8  7
♦  K  9  7  6
♣  8  7  6
```

you would bid 1♠. If partner rebids 2♡ you should pass. Partner has a long heart suit and a minimum hand.

If, at your second turn as responder, you have a good hand but don't know where the hand should be played, you can force partner to bid again by bidding a new suit. A new suit by responder is forcing when NT has not been bid.

If you have
```
♠  A  Q  5  4  3
♥  A  K  5  4
♦  2
♣  6  4  2
```

and partner opened 1◊, you bid 1♠, and partner rebids 2◊, what do you bid? You have an opening hand so you will want to be in game.

AN OPENING HAND OPPOSITE AN OPENING HAND BELONGS IN GAME SOMEWHERE

The problem in this hand is you still don't know where; spades, hearts or NT seem most likely. You next bid 2♡, which partner cannot pass. If he has four hearts, he should raise hearts. If he has three spades, he should bid spades. (He has already denied having four spades when he didn't raise them immediately.) If he has neither of these, he would bid NT if he has some honors in clubs. If he bids 2NT, you bid 3NT.

Very often however, you will know where the hand should be played when it's time for your second bid. Then your job is to keep the bidding at a low level with weak hands, invite a game with middle-of-the-road hands, or bid game with enough count for game. Occasionally, of course, you will even try for a slam. If partner opened 1◇ and you have

♠ A 8 4 3
♥ K 8 7 5
♦ 4
♣ A Q 5 4

bid 1♥. With four hearts and four spades, respond with 1♥, regardless of quality. If partner rebids 1♠, bid 4♠. Partner must have a four-card spade suit, which gives you eight spades. It is your second turn to bid, you have an opening hand and you know what suit should be trump. Bid the game!!

QUIZ

1. If opener rebids his own suit, it shows a minimum hand of ___ to ___ points.
2. If opener raises partner's suit from 1 to 2 (1♣—1♥—2♥) it shows from ___ to ___ points.
3. If opener rebids 1NT, it shows ___ to ___ HCP.
4. A rebid of a suit without a raise from partner always shows at least ___ cards of the suit.
5. An opening hand opposite an opening hand should be in ___ somewhere.
6. If responder has an opening hand, at his second turn he must either bid game or make a ___ bid.

Your partner has opened 1♣. You respond 1♥. Partner rebids 1♠. Plan your next bid with each of these hands.

7. ♠ A 4 3 2	8. ♠ 4 3	9. ♠ A 4 3 2
♥ Q 4 3 2	♥ A K 7 6 3 2	♥ Q 9 5 3
♦ A 4 3	♦ 8 7 2	♦ Q 2
♣ A 2	♣ 9 8	♣ K 3 2

Your partner has opened 1♠. You respond 2♣. Partner rebids 2♡. Plan your next bid with each of these hands.

10. ♠ 3 2
    ♥ A 4 3 2
    ♦ 3 2
    ♣ A K Q 4 3

11. ♠ 5 4
    ♥ 6 5
    ♦ A K 4 3
    ♣ A Q 4 3 2

12. ♠ 4 3
    ♥ Q 2
    ♦ 8 7 6
    ♣ A K Q 4 3 2

Answers

1.   13-15/16
2.   13-15/16
3.   12-14
4.   5, usually 6 cards.
5.   Game
6.   Forcing
7.   4♠. You have an opening hand and it's your second turn.
8.   2♡
9.   3♠. Near opener
10. 4♡. You have an opening hand and it's your second turn.
11. 3 NT. You have an opening hand and it's your second turn.
12. 3♣. If partner now bids 3NT, you should pass.

Chapter SIX
OPENING WITH LARGE HANDS

Occasionally you pick up a hand that is so good that you feel you want to be in game, even though partner's hand may not be good enough to make a simple response if you were to open one of a suit. These hands are opened with two of a suit. This is a GAME-FORCING bid. There are several reasons why you don't simply open the bidding with a game bid with a very large hand. One is that you frequently need partner's help in selecting the suit that will work best as trump (or possibly a NT contract); another is that if you leave some bidding space for partner, you may find that he has just what you need for slam.

If you picked up   ♠   A   K   5   4   3
                             ♥   A   K   6   5   4
                             ♦   A   K   J
                             ♣   —   —   —

you have 22 HCP, two good five-card suits—both majors, lots of aces and kings, and a void. A beautiful hand! You are heavily favored to make a game somewhere; it would be sad to have to guess at the best game contract and guess wrong. And, if partner has the right stuff in the right places, you could easily have a slam. Open with 2♠. If partner doesn't raise spades, you'll try hearts next. Partner will know that you are in a game-forcing auction and will keep making descriptive bids until you get to game—some days a slam. In general, you need a bit more to open with 2 of a minor than with 2 of a major. If you open 2 of a minor and your hand is not suitable for notrump, you will have to play in 5 of a minor, which is harder to make than 4 of a major.

An opening bid of two of a suit is made with a hand that you can count enough tricks for a game, or within one trick of game, or a hand that has about 22/23 or more points. The hand could be big enough that there is a slam. The suit that you open with a strong two-bid should have five or more cards.

1. ♠ A K Q 6 5 4 2   2. ♠ A K J   3. ♠ A K 7 4 3 2
    ♥ A K 3 2   ♥ A K 7 4 2   ♥ A K Q J 3
    ♦ 2   ♦ A Q J 2   ♦ A 2
    ♣ 3   ♣ 2   ♣ — — —

1. Open with 2♠. There are probably seven spade tricks and two sure heart tricks. There are numerous hands with which you can make game if partner has very few or even no HCP points. An opening bid of 4♠ is saved for hands with a very long suit, such as an eight-card suit, with very few high cards outside the trump suit.

2. Open with 2♡. You have 22 HCP and enough positive features, "perks," that give extra value. There is too much of a chance that partner has enough for you to make a game somewhere without having enough points to bid over a 1♡ opening.

3. Bid 2♠. Never lose sight of the fact that partner can't pass. Partner would bid 2NT with a very weak hand (0 to 6). If partner should raise your spades, he has some points and 3 or more spades. Now you move your thoughts from game to slam. Partner has three or more spades so you rate to lose no spades. A small slam should be easy, maybe a grand, but it's best not to chance a grand at this point. As you learn more tools, there will be more information to help make final decisions.

With the first hand, if partner bids 3♠, you should be *very* interested in slam. However, you are missing aces in both minor suits. You ask for aces in the following method. After the 3♠ bid you now bid 4NT, which is an ace-asking bid called Blackwood.

	Responses		
4NT (asks for aces)	5♣	=	0 (or 4)
	5♢	=	1
	5♡	=	2
	5♠	=	3

If responder answers 5♣, you stop in 5♠. If partner bids 5♢ or 5♡, bid 6♠. Granted if he answers 5♡, showing 2 aces, you might make a grand slam, but greed could be costly. It's OK to bid a small slam that looks promising, but to bid a grand slam you need to be *quite certain that there are no losers.* Better to be in 6 and make 7 than to be in 7 and make 6.

Responder is forced to bid until game is reached, even with *no* points. Remember, opener wants to be in game, or possibly slam. Responder's job is to help find the best spot. Since responder is forced to bid, it becomes necessary to have ways of showing some values and bids that show weak hands.

A hand with 7 or more points in high cards or counting distribution, if you can raise partner's suit, is considered a good hand. There are two weak responses (less than 7 points) after partner has opened with two of a suit.

1. A response of 2NT is weak. It may or may not be a balanced hand. It merely shows a weak hand.
2. A raise of partner's suit to game shows a weak hand. It shows fairly good trump support, usually four of them with at least one honor (QJ43, Q752), with little or nothing else. The jump to 4♠ is an attempt to slow partner down; but remember, his hand is unlimited so he will bid a slam if all he needs is trump support. If partner opened with 2♠, a raise to 3♠ is a stronger bid than a raise to 4♠. The reason for this is that with good values, it is better to leave more bidding room to be able to communicate more information in case there may be a slam.

All bids, other than 2NT or a direct raise to game, show hands with 7 or more points. Partner opens with 2♡ and you have

1.	♠	Q 7 6 4 2		2.	♠	10 2
	♥	4			♥	Q 7 4 2
	♦	8 7 4			♦	4 3 2
	♣	9 5 3 2			♣	8 4 3 2

1. Bid 2NT. Bidding a new suit shows 7+ points and five or more cards in the suit. 2NT is an artificial bid saying that you have a weak hand. If partner rebids 3♡, you now bid 3♠. Partner now knows that you have a weak hand and a long spade suit.
2. Bid 4♡. Your hand is weak. This bid says, "Partner, you wanted to be in game and I have reasonably good trumps but nothing more to contribute." A bid of 3♡ would be used for hands with which you want to leave room to communicate to determine if the hands fit well so that you might be able to make slam. It would also show 7+ points.

One other strong opening bid available is a bid of 2NT. It shows 22-24 HCP and is balanced. This bid is not forcing, but if responder has as many as 3 points, game should be bid; there are about 26 points between the two hands. In this case, there is no room to invite game, so assume partner is in the middle (23). Therefore, if as responder, you have 3 points, the partnership has 26 points and you should be in game.

Opening 3NT shows a balanced hand of 25-26-27 HCP.

PRACTICE HAND

North
- ♠ J 3 2
- ♥ 3
- ♦ J 5 4 3
- ♣ 7 6 5 4 2

West
- ♠ 10 4
- ♥ K 8 7 6 2
- ♦ 8 7
- ♣ K Q J 3

East
- ♠ 8 7 6
- ♥ Q J 10 5 4
- ♦ A 10 9 2
- ♣ 10

South
- ♠ A K Q 9 5
- ♥ A 9
- ♦ K Q 6
- ♣ A 9 8

THE AUCTION

North	East	South	West
Pass	Pass	2♠	Pass
2NT	Pass	3NT	Pass
4♠	Pass	Pass	Pass

West selects the ♣K as the opening lead. (Without touching honors he would lead fourth best.) Declarer wins with the A. Although it's important to pull trumps early, with this hand, you need to trump a heart in dummy first. Play the ace of hearts and trump a heart, then pull trump. Notice, if you play three rounds of trumps first you will have no trumps left in dummy with which to trump your little heart. Finish the play of this hand.

QUIZ

1. An opening bid of 2♡ is game-forcing. ___ T/F
2. An opening bid of 2NT is game-forcing. ___ T/F
3. A 2NT response to a 2♠ opener is weak. ___ T/F
4. A 4♡ response to a 2♡ opener is weak with good trumps. ___ T/F
5. A 2◇ opening bid shows ___ or more cards in the diamond suit.
6. If you open with 2♡ you either have a lot of points, or you can count ___ or more tricks in your hand.
7. For a 2◇ opener, you would need a bit better hand than to open with 2 of a major. ___ T/F
8. After a 2♣ opening bid, a response of 2♡ shows ___ or more points.
9. After a 2♡ opening, a response of 3♡ shows ___ or more points.
10. An opening bid of 2NT shows ___ to ___ HCP.

What do you open with these hands?

11. ♠ A K 10 9 5 3
     ♥ 2
     ♦ A K Q 10
     ♣ A 7

12. ♠ 2
     ♥ J 10 8 7 2
     ♦ A K 7
     ♣ A K Q J

13. ♠ A 7 6
     ♥ A K
     ♦ K Q 6 5 2
     ♣ K Q J

14. ♠ A K J
     ♥ K Q 10 3 2
     ♦ A K Q 2
     ♣ 3

ANSWERS

1. True
2. False
3. True
4. True
5. 5
6. 9
7. True
8. 7
9. 7
10. 22-24

11. 2♠. The sixth spade in your hand makes that suit have five probable winners. The hand has nine or more winners.
12. 1♡. You intend to make a strong rebid if partner responds.
13. 2NT. If partner is broke, you are high enough.
14. 2♡

PAGE OF PERKS

Point-count bidding is a useful tool for evaluating the size of a hand. It is especially good for notrump bidding. For a long time we have been aware that 4-3-2-1 points for ace through jack is not as accurate as we'd like, because it underrates the ace and somewhat overrates queens and jacks when they are not combined with other honors. Oswald Jacoby, a personal hero of mine, once proposed the idea of fractions. It was, without a doubt, a more accurate assessment of the trick-taking capability of these cards, but we can only imagine the length of time it would take for people to count their points.

Then comes the question of assessing unbalanced hands. There have been dozens of ideas as to what credit should be given for long suits and short suits and, as typical, not any one method is perfect. What is kind of entertaining is that people tend to get locked into their ways of counting, when in fact most methods come out about the same, even if the means of arriving at a certain number may be different. One thing that people tend to agree upon is when your side has picked a trump suit, a short suit, such as a singleton, is clearly valuable, so we add 2 or 3 points depending on the conditions. Those points are every bit as valuable as our HCP.

In addition to our points, it is valuable to look at "perks." I like the idea of perks, because otherwise you can add and subtract points until your head feels like it's swimming. When you need to use the perks is in close decisions about something: Should I open? Should I accept partner's invitation to game? Should I be thinking of a slam? etc.

The following is a list of assets or perks. Some people assign a point for some of these and others simply like to be aware of the many things worthy of note after counting "raw" points. The perks are not listed in any specific order of importance.

PERKS

1. Good supply of quick tricks.
2. Honors in long suits.
3. Honors together.
4. A strong five-card suit.
   Some routinely add a point for this and that is reasonable.
5. A strong six-card suit (BIG perk).
6. Good fillers—J1098 rather than J432.
7. Length in majors.
8. A double-suit fit with partner (BIG perk).
9. Two-suited hands—with strength in both of the long suits (BIG perk).
10. With a long and very strong suit you can begin counting tricks rather than points. The following suit is favored to take 8 tricks.
    AK876432 - Assigning points to this suit wouldn't do it justice.
11. **Four-card support for partner's five-card major opening.**
    I confess I like adding a point for this.
12. A singleton.
13. A Void.

Concerning 12 & 13:
Long suits and short suits go hand in hand, but even a hand with no long suits, such as 4-4-4-1 distribution, has more playing potential than 4-3-3-3, or even 4-4-3-2. The discussions on what things are valuable are often a question of semantics. My preference is to assign points to a singleton or void after a trump suit has been found. In the meantime, it is a perk.

FLAWS

1. Very flat hands. 4,3,3,3 distribution.
2. Honors in short suits.
3. Most of your points tied up in queens and jacks.
4. Misfit with partner.
5. Grumpy partners.

One of the most important considerations in bidding is to know which bids are forcing and which bids can be passed. A forcing bid is one which partner cannot pass at the next turn. Some bids are forcing all the way to game and some are forcing only for one round. Since there are so many possible auctions, a few generalizations are necessary. We learned in Chapter V that when we know where a contract should be played and that there are enough points for game, at our second bid we should bid the game, either as opener or responder. Forcing bids are needed when we don't know as yet where a contract should be played.

THE MOST COMMON FORCING BID BY OPENER IS A JUMP SHIFT: 1♡—1♠—3♣. The 3♣ bid shows 19+ points; it is *game*-forcing because with the 6 points guaranteed by responder, there are enough points for game. If you open this hand with 1♡ and partner responds 1♠, you need to rebid 3♣, as partner could pass 2♣.

       ♠ A 4
       ♥ K Q J 7 4
       ♦ 5 3
       ♣ A K Q 2

You want to be in game with this hand even if partner has only 6-7 points, but at this moment you don't know where.

Opener's rebid of a new suit is not forcing: 1♡—1♠—2♣ (the opponents are passing). It doesn't even guarantee extra values. It would show a hand of five or more hearts, and four or more clubs, and from 13-18 points. Notice that it may be more than a minimum, but denies as many as 19.

Opener's rebid of a jump to 2NT is also game-forcing.

South	West	North	East
1◇	Pass	1♡	Pass
2NT			

The 2NT bid shows a balanced hand that was too big to open 1NT. It shows 19, 20 or 21 points. If you hold

♠ A K J
♥ K 3 2
♦ A J 5 4 3
♣ K 2

and the auction has gone 1♢—1♡—2NT as in the last auction, if partner rebids 3♡, you would raise to 4♡, as partner's rebidding them would guarantee five or more hearts (most of the time when responder rebids his suit it shows 6 cards, but when you bid NT he can rebid a 5-card suit.) If partner bids 3♣ over your 2NT, you should bid 3♡ next. This will show a three-card heart suit. If you had four of them, you would have raised immediately over 1♡. Partner will not pass anything short of game, as your 2NT rebid was game-forcing.

If opener jumps in his own suit or in partner's, it shows extra values, (about 17 points), but it is not forcing. Responder could pass with only 6-7, but should bid with more than 7. If the bidding had gone 1♣ by you, as opener, and you have

♠ A Q 4 3
♥ 2
♦ A 4 2
♣ K Q 5 4 3

and if partner responded 1♠, you would rebid 3♠. This would say that you have a very nice hand, about 17 points (good 16, 17, 18) and have a definite interest in game, but you can't do it by yourself. Note that if you had any more points, say another Q, which would give you 20 points, you would bid game directly. One other point on this hand: to rebid your club suit would be unthinkable. It's much more important to let your partner know you have found a major suit to have as trump than to tell about your five-card club suit.

Suppose you open 1♢ with the following hand

♠ A 7 6 5
♥ 9
♦ A K Q 6 4
♣ K Q 2

After you open with 1♢, your partner responds 1♠. What is your rebid as opener? Now that you have found a trump suit, you count everything (HCP and distribution). Bid a direct 4♠. This bid shows 19-20-21 points. Remember, any jump by opener shows a strong hand.

Suppose there is a slam! The responder knows that opener has about 20 points. If responder has a hand such as

♠ K Q 3 2
♥ K 8 7
♦ 3 2
♣ A 9 8 2

it is responder who knows that slam is likely. He should bid 4NT, and if opener shows 2 or 3 aces responder should bid 6♠.

RESPONDER HAS MANY FORCING BIDS. We have already learned that immediate jumps are forcing, 1♥—3♥, or 1♥—2NT; and, of course, a jump shift, 1◇—2♠, is forcing. These are all game-forcing bids, as they announce opening hands or better.

After partner's opening bid of one of a suit, a new suit by responder is forcing, 1◇—1♠, as the point range for this bid is 6-18 points. **A two-over-one bid,** 1♥—2◇, **is, of course, forcing as it shows at least 10-18 points.** Since a new suit bid by responder can be on as few as 6 points (on the one level) or could be big, it is forcing for one round. Responder will usually jump-shift with as many as 19 points, but doesn't have to if, for example, he doesn't have a five-card suit. Occasionally, therefore, the new suit bid by responder will actually be more than 18 points.

Responder's new suit bids below the game level are forcing even at later turns if NT has not been bid. In the auction

| 1♣ | (Pass) | 1◇ | (Pass) |
| 1♥ | (Pass) | 1♠ | 1♠ is forcing, |

or

| 1♣ | (Pass) | 1♥ | (Pass) |
| 2♣ | (Pass) | 2◇ | 2◇ is forcing. |

For the latter auction, your hand might be

♠ 4 2
♥ A K 9 7 6
♦ A K 5 3
♣ 9 8

You know you want to be in game, as you have an opener opposite an opener, but you are not in a position to decide where. This is the reason that new suits by responder need to be forcing.

If NT has been bid, such as,

| 1◇ | (Pass) | 1♠ | (Pass) |
| 1NT | (Pass) | 2♣ | |

2♣ is not forcing because NT has been bid.

You would have to jump to 3♣ to force. This is to allow you to play in a suit at a low level if your hand is weak. Partner's 1NT rebid shows a balanced hand with 12, 13, or 14 HCP. If you hold the following

```
♠  A  7  6  5  2
♥  4
♦  4  3
♣  K  9  7  3  2
```

you would like to have either spades or clubs as trump rather than play in NT, but you don't want to be very high as your hand is weak. Partner could pass your 2♣ bid or could bid 2♠ if he likes spades better than clubs.

If an auction proceeds

| 1♡ | (Pass) | 1NT | (Pass) |
| 2♣ | (Pass) | 2◇ | |

2◇ is not forcing, because the original 1NT limited the hand to 6-10 HCP. This is a hand that you would have bid 2◇ at your first response, but your hand wasn't good enough for a two-over-one bid, such as

```
♠  6  5  4
♥  4
♦  A  Q  5  4  3  2
♣  6  4  2
```

If responder, at his second turn, jumps in opener's suit, it is not forcing

| 1◇ | Pass | 1♡ | Pass |
| 1♠ | Pass | 3♠ | |

because when responder knows where the contract is going to be played (spades) if he has enough points for game, at his second bid, he should bid the game himself. In the above auction, the 3♠ bid shows nearly an opening hand, such as

♠ A 4 3 2
♥ K 8 7 4
♦ 5 4
♣ K 3 2

You want to be in game, unless partner is on a very minimum opener.

Responder's jump in his own suit, however, shows an opening hand with a long suit and is forcing. If you held this hand, after partner's 1◊ opening, you would bid 1♡

♠ A 3
♥ A K 7 6 5 3
♦ Q 5
♣ 7 6 5

and if partner rebid 2◊, you should jump to 3♡. You know that you want to be in game, but you are not in a position to bid it as you don't know, as yet, where it should be played.

There are certain conditions in which bids have a different meaning. Once you have passed you are known to have less than 13 points, so most previously forcing bids are no longer forcing. Examine the following auctions:

North	East	South	West
Pass	Pass	1♠	Pass
3♠			

or

North	East	South	West
Pass	Pass	1♡	Pass
2◊			

North's bid of 3♠ shows a near opener, 11-12 points, with spade support. In the second example, the 2◊ bidder is known to have less than an opening hand.

As a *passed* hand, raises of partner's heart suit are:

2♡ = 6-10
3♡ = 11-12
4♡ = 13+ The hand grew because of distribution.

Again, when partner opens after you have previously passed, if you have a hand with which you want to be in game because your hand fits well, you must bid game directly.

If you held this hand   ♠   A   5   4   2
                        ♥   3
                        ♦   K   Q   J   2
                        ♣   8   7   4   2

and the bidding has gone pass by you, pass by your LHO, 1♠ by partner, pass by RHO, the only way of ensuring getting to game is by bidding 4♠. Even a new suit bid by you would not be forcing after you have passed.

If your side has a part score, there are added inferences drawn if partner bids beyond what you need to make a game. Suppose you have a 40 part score and have the following auction: you open 1♡ and partner bids 3♡. His 3♡ bid would normally be forcing, but you will complete your game by making 3♡, so now it isn't forcing. However, 2♡ would have been enough for game, so why did partner bid 3♡? He must be suggesting a slam. If your hand is a minimum, you should pass, but if you have extra values, you might investigate a slam.

A RECOMMENDATION which prevents many bidding problems: When partner has opened and you change suits on the two level, such as 1♠ (Pass) 2♣, if partner limits his hand by rebidding 2NT you can pass. If he changes suits or rebids his suit, you promise another bid. For example, 1♠ (Pass) 2♣ (Pass) 2♠, you are expected to bid again.

A More Advanced Bidding Point: One other forcing bid by opener, which is standard among very experienced bridge players, is a *reverse*.

South	West	North	East
1◇	Pass	1♠	Pass
2♡			

The second suit bid by opener is higher-ranking than the first suit and it is on the two level. This bid takes up a lot of bidding room. If partner should happen to be short in hearts but has some diamonds, he would have to bid on the three level to return to your first-bid suit. For you to be willing for the auction to get that high, you should have a big hand, such as

♠ A 8 7
♥ A K J 3
♦ A J 10 7 3
♣ 7

For more information on Reverses, see *Later in the Auction Vol. II* in the BRIDGE Mini Series. See the back of the book for a complete list of titles.

Recap for Common Forcing Bids if you are below the game level:

FORCING 1ST BIDS BY RESPONDER
New Suit Bid
Jump in Partner's Suit
Jump Shift
Jump to 2NT

FORCING REBIDS BY OPENER
Jump Shift
Jump to 2NT
A Reverse

FORCING 2ND BIDS BY RESPONDER
NEW SUIT if NT has not been bid;
if 1NT has been bid, such as a 1NT rebid
by opener, a jump would be needed to force.
A Jump in Your Own Suit

When the opponents interfere in your auction, there is the additional forcing bid available of cue bidding the opponent's suit. This shows a big hand and is forcing to game.

Also, new suits are forcing when a previously bid suit has been supported, such as 1♡—2♡—3♣.

QUIZ

Which of the underlined bids are forcing:

	Opener	Responder		Opener	Responder
1.	1♡	<u>1NT</u>	12.	1♡	1♠
2.	1♠	<u>2NT</u>		<u>3♣</u>	
3.	1◇	<u>1♡</u>	13.	1♡	1♠
4.	1♠	<u>2♣</u>		2◇	<u>2♠</u>
5.	1◇	<u>2♠</u>	14.	1♣	1♡
6.	1◇	<u>3NT</u>		2♣	<u>3♣</u>
7.	1♡	1♠	15.	1♡	1♠
	<u>2♠</u>			2♡	<u>2NT</u>
8.	1♡	1♠	16.	1♡	1♠
	<u>3♠</u>			2♡	<u>3♣</u>
9.	1♣	1♡	17.	1♡	1NT
	<u>2NT</u>			2♣	<u>2◇</u>
10.	1◇	1♡	18.	1◇	<u>1♠</u>
	<u>3◇</u>			2◇	<u>3♠</u>
11.	1♣	1♠			
	<u>4♠</u>				

ANSWERS

2, 3, 4, 5, 9, 12, 16, 18.

Chapter EIGHT
OVERCALLS

An overcall is a bid of a suit or NT made after an opponent has opened the auction. Typically when you overcall at the one or two level, you will have about 11/12 – 17 HCP and a long, strong suit.

Your hand:

♠ A Q 2
♥ A K 9 7 5
♦ 8 5 3
♣ 9 8

You are getting ready to open 1♡ when the dealer, on your right opens 1◇. No problem. You simply overcall 1♡. However, if the dealer opens 1♠ you will be at the two level, but this is not a problem either. You overcall 2♡.

With the next hand you were about to open 1◇

♠ A 3
♥ K 10 9 4
♦ K 9 7 4
♣ K 9 5

when your RHO (right-hand opponent) opens 1♡. Now you have a problem. Remember that an overcall shows a **long** suit, which you don't have. Overcalling a four-card suit on the two level (and your suit isn't strong either) is sinful. Don't do it. Ever. In the next chapter there is a complete explanation about a way to enter the auction with a takeout double. In that chapter you will find that your hand isn't right for that bid either. Sad, but you must pass. If partner, on his own initiative makes a bid, you then might do something dramatic, such as jump to game. For example, if you pass, LHO passes and partner bids 2♣, at your next turn you could bid 3NT.

There is some difference between overcalling at the one level and the two level. At the one level you can have as few as 10 HCP if your suit is both long and strong. Unless your suit is good there is no reason to overcall with only 10 points. Most of the time your hand will be an opening hand or very close. In general don't overcall with a poor suit unless your hand is quite good. **At the two level you want it all—a long, strong suit and an opening hand.**

Your RHO opens 1◇ and you have the following hands:

1. ♠ K J 4
    ♥ A K 10 6 5
    ♦ 7 4 3
    ♣ 5 4

2. ♠ A 3
    ♥ J 7 5 4 2
    ♦ Q 5 4
    ♣ K 6 2

3. ♠ A Q 8 6 4
    ♥ A K 9 7 5
    ♦ 6
    ♣ 8 7

4. ♠ A 6
    ♥ J 7 5 4 2
    ♦ A 6 5
    ♣ A Q 5

1. Bid 1♡. You have a near opener, 11 HCP, and a good five-card heart suit.
2. Pass. Your hand is minimal and your suit is bad.
3. Bid 1 ♠. If partner doesn't raise spades, you intend to bid hearts next.
4. Bid 1 ♡. Your suit isn't good, but your hand is so good it's hard to pass.

When the opponents bid your longest suit, you should usually pass *smoothly,* unless you are able to overcall 1NT. A NT overcall shows a fairly balanced hand of 15-16 up to 18 points with the opening bid suit well stopped. If the opponent has opened 1♠ and you have

1. ♠ A Q 5 4 3
    ♥ K 7 6
    ♦ A 4
    ♣ 6 5 4

2. ♠ A J 3
    ♥ K 6 5
    ♦ K J 7 2
    ♣ K Q 4

3. ♠ A Q 4
    ♥ 4 2
    ♦ K Q 4 2
    ♣ Q 7 6 2

1. Pass—smoothly.
2. Overcall 1NT.
3. Pass. One hates to pass with 13 HCP, but you have no better choice. You were going to open 1◊. Although the opponents didn't bid your suit, they deprived you of bidding it at the one level. You should never overcall a four-card suit at the two level.

There are times when it is reasonable to overcall on a four-card suit at the one level. If your RHO opened 1◊ and you had

    ♠ A K Q 2
    ♥ 5 3
    ♦ 8 6 4
    ♣ A J 10 2

you would feel rather justified in bidding 1♠ with this strong four-card suit. These situations occur infrequently. Your partner should still assume that your overcall shows a five-card suit because almost always it will be.

RESPONDING TO OVERCALLS

The general theory in responding to an overcall is that you should bid as much as you think you can make. Anytime you have enough points and three-or-more-card support of your partner's suit, you can raise, since partner presumably has a five-card suit. **A raise of partner's overcall from one to two shows 6-10 points, including distribution. A raise to three shows 11-12 points, and is not forcing. A raise to game shows 13 or more.** Remember, distribution is counted full value.

With no fit for partner's suit, you should usually pass with 6-7 or even 8 points. If you have the opponent's suit well covered and your hand is suitable for NT, bid 1NT with 8-10 points, 2NT with 11-12, and 3NT with 13 or more. If you have three or more cards of partner's major, it is better to stay with the major rather than bidding NT. Bidding your own suit after partner has overcalled is not forcing but promises five or six cards in the suit and about 10 HCP, give or take a point or two; never fewer than five cards.

If your opponent bids 1♡, your partner overcalls 1♠, and you have:

1. ♠ A 3
    ♥ A J 4
    ♦ K 5 4 3
    ♣ 6 5 4 2

2. ♠ A 5 4
   ♥ A 6 5
   ♦ Q 7 6 5 3
   ♣ 5 4

3. ♠ A 6 5
    ♥ 5 4 3
    ♦ K 4
    ♣ A Q 7 6 5

4. ♠ 3 2
   ♥ 7 6 4
   ♦ Q 5 4
   ♣ K Q 6 5 4

1. Bid 2NT.
2. Bid 3♠.
3. Bid 4♠; remember, 2♣ isn't forcing.
4. Pass. You have only 7 points so you have no need to bid.

There are different ways of playing single jump overcalls, such as jumping to 2♠ or 3♣ over an opponent's 1◇ opening. In the past, the most common way of playing the single jump overcall was that it showed a hand stronger than an overcall, or roughly 18-21 or 22 points. A double jump has always been preemptive.

The current trend is to play **ALL JUMP OVERCALLS AS WEAK.**

This would mean that a 1◇ opener by the opponents and a 2♠ bid by you would be weak—a good six-card suit meaning 2 to 3 honors in the suit and not much outside—about 6-10 HCP. The consistency makes it easier to remember and the preemptive bid is very effective. It is my recommendation to play this latter style, but make sure you and your partner have this agreement to avoid misunderstandings. See Chapter 16.

As a matter of clarity, this style or treatment is called WEAK JUMP OVERCALLS, not weak two-bids. Weak two-bids refer to opening bids, not to overcalls.

QUIZ

Your right-hand opponent opens with 1♡ and you have

1. ♠ 9 7 5 3 2	2. ♠ A K Q 6 5	3. ♠ 7 6
♥ A 6 5	♥ 7 6	♥ Q 4 3
♦ A Q 4	♦ Q 4 3	♦ J 9 8 7 4
♣ 5 4	♣ 6 5 2	♣ A K J

4. ♠ A 3	5. ♠ J 9 8 7 4	
♥ A Q 6 5 4	♥ A 8	
♦ K 8 7	♦ A K 8 7	
♣ 8 7 5	♣ K 4	What are your bids?

This time, your left-hand opponent opened 1♢. Your partner has overcalled 1♠ and the next player passed. You have:

6. ♠ 7 6 5 3
    ♥ A 7 6
    ♦ 2
    ♣ A 8 7 5 3

7. ♠ 7 6 4
    ♥ 9 7 3 2
    ♦ A 8 7 6
    ♣ K 2

8. ♠ 5 4
    ♥ 7 5 4
    ♦ A Q 7 6
    ♣ A 8 7 4

9. ♠ 8 6 4 3
    ♥ 2
    ♦ A 8 7 6
    ♣ A K 7 6

10. ♠ 8 6
    ♥ Q 6 5
    ♦ A 7 5 3
    ♣ 8 6 4 3

11. ♠ 5 2
    ♥ A 6 3
    ♦ A Q 8 7
    ♣ A 7 6 3

12. ♠ Q 8 7 6 3
    ♥ — — —
    ♦ 9 8 7 4
    ♣ A Q 6 5

13. ♠ 4
    ♥ A K 8 6 3 2
    ♦ 9 7
    ♣ J 7 6 3

14. ♠ 7 6
    ♥ A 8 7
    ♦ K J 10
    ♣ K 10 9 6 4

15. ♠ 8 5 2
    ♥ 6 5
    ♦ 8 7 5
    ♣ A K 7 6 5   What are your bids?

ANSWERS

1. Pass
2. 1♠
3. Pass
4. Pass—When the opponents bid your longest suit, pass smoothly.
5. 1♠
6. 3♠—invitational.
7. 2♠—You have three cards and your partner is known to have five.
8. 1NT
9. 4♠

10. Pass
11. 3NT
12. 4♠—With so many trump, count 5 points for the void; your hand evaluates to 13 points.
13. 2♥
14. 2NT
15. 2♠—Avoid bidding 2♣ as that isn't forcing, and you already know that you have at least eight cards in spades.

Chapter NINE
TAKEOUT DOUBLES

A bid of "double" has more than one meaning in bridge. It is sometimes used as a penalty double, which is for the purpose of increasing the points you receive if the opponents fail to make a contract. If the opponents bid their way to 4♠ and you think you can defeat the contract, you would double. If you are right, you will reap the rewards.

There is another common meaning of the double. A *takeout* double is used as a request for partner to bid. His job is to pick the trump suit. If your RHO opened with 1◇ and you have

♠ A 8 6 4

♥ K J 7 6

♦ 4

♣ A J 6 5

you would like to be able to bid with this hand, but you have no five-card suit to overcall. Actually you have three fairly good suits. You should double with this hand, which tells partner to pick the trump suit from one of the three unbid suits. Whichever he picks will be okay with you. Once he picks the trump suit, your singleton will add a couple of points to this hand.

It is always a pleasant experience to know what partner's bids mean and for partner to have some idea as to the meaning of your bids. A double which is intended for "takeout" as opposed to penalty is used in specific situations.

A takeout double is made at your first opportunity to double the suit bid, PARTNER HAS EITHER PASSED OR NOT HAD AN OPPORTUNITY TO BID, and it must be below the game level. It shows an opening hand or better and the hand should contain three or *four* cards in each of the unbid suits, as partner is asked to pick one of "your" suits as trump.

An exception can be made to the distributional requirement if the hand has substantial extra values.

When an opponent opens the bidding with a preemptive bid at the three-level, a double of that bid also is for takeout.

Examine the following auctions to determine which of the following doubles are takeout and which are penalty.

	North	East	South	West
1.	1♡	Dbl		
2.	1♡	Pass	1NT	Pass
	2♡	Dbl		
3.	1♠	2◇	Dbl	
4.	1NT	Pass	4♠	Dbl
5.	1◇	Pass	1♠	Dbl
6.	3◇	Dbl		

1. Takeout
2. Penalty. It was not the first opportunity to double this suit.
3. Penalty. Partner has made a bid. In the absence of any agreed-upon conventions, this double says, I have good diamonds and expect to beat this contract by a couple of tricks.
4. Penalty. The opponents are at the game level.
5. Takeout. Partner has not bid and it is your first opportunity to double. Since the opponents have bid two suits, your double shows the remaining two suits, hearts and clubs.
6. Takeout.

Consider the following hands after your RHO opens with 1◇

1. ♠ A 6 5 4
   ♥ A J 5
   ♦ 7 6
   ♣ K J 7 6

2. ♠ A
   ♥ K 4 3 2
   ♦ 8 7 6 5
   ♣ A Q 7 6

3. ♠ A 8 7 6
   ♥ A 5 4 2
   ♦ 4
   ♣ K 8 4 3

4. ♠ A J 8 7 6
   ♥ Q 6 5
   ♦ 6 5
   ♣ A Q 5

1. This is a good takeout double. If partner bids any of the other three suits, you have support.

2. Pass. You don't have spades. You need to have support for any suit partner might bid.
3. Double. This is a minimum for a takeout double, but it qualifies.
4. Bid 1♠. This qualifies for a double, but with a good five-card suit, it is better to bid your suit, especially when it is a major suit.

When partner has made a takeout double, unless your RHO bids, you are basically forced to bid. If you don't, you will turn your partner's takeout double into penalty by your pass. If partner has made a takeout double of 1♡ with this hand

♠ A 6 3 2	and you have	♠ 9 7 3 2
♥ 5		♥ 8 7 4 3
♦ A 8 6 5		♦ J 3 2
♣ A 9 3 2		♣ K 6

it may seem that you would like to pass, but consider the consequences. If you pass, your side will presumably take four tricks. This means the opponents will make their contract—1♡ doubled = 60, plus 50 for the insult, plus 100 or 200 for each overtrick that they make, depending on vulnerability. You would lose about 300 to 500 points. If you pick the trump suit, as requested, you may not make it, but the penalty would surely not be so severe.

When partner has made a takeout double and the next person passes, the only time you pass is when you want to defend. You have five or more very good cards in the opponents' suit and a fairly good hand. If partner makes a takeout double of 1 ♠, you would pass with

	♠ A K J 10 8
	♥ A 6 5
	♦ 7 6 5
	♣ 6 5

You are happy to defend 1 ♠ doubled and expect a handsome profit. If the opponents try to escape to a new suit, partner very likely will be able to double that.

Unless you have the rare hand with which you are willing to defend because you expect to set the opponents,

> YOU MUST BID OVER PARTNER'S TAKEOUT DOUBLE,
> REGARDLESS OF HOW BAD YOUR HAND IS.

Since you are basically forced to bid, it is important to distinguish between hands with which you are glad to bid and hands that you are bidding only because you must. If partner makes a takeout double of 1◇, consider these two hands.

1. ♠ 5 4 3 2   2. ♠ Q 7 6 5 4
   ♥ 6 4   ♥ 4 3 2
   ♦ K J 6   ♦ A K 2
   ♣ 5 4 3 2   ♣ 3 2

If you bid 1♠ with each of these hands, partner would not know when to bid again. **Since you were forced to bid, you need to distinguish between bad hands and good hands.** Therefore, responding to a takeout double must be different than responding to partner's opening bid:

■ **A bid of a suit at the cheapest level shows 0-8 points**
■ **A one-level jump equals 9-11 points**
■ **And hands of about opening strength are bid directly to game.**

You would bid 1♠ with the first hand above, and bid 2♠ with the second.

Your partner has made a takeout double, asking you to pick the trump suit. Nevertheless, you may have some hands with which notrump seems like the best spot. Since partner's hand is more oriented towards suit play when he makes the takeout double, your notrump responses should be made on fairly good hands.

In response to a takeout double,

> ■ **With 8-10 HCP and the opponent's suit well stopped, bid 1NT.**
> ■ **With 11-12 HCP and the opponent's suit well stopped, bid 2NT.**
> ■ **With 13 or more points and the opponent's suit well stopped, bid 3NT.**

If you have four or more cards in a major, bid that suit in preference to notrump; and, as usual, try to pick a major suit over a minor suit.

A DOUBLE OF A 1NT OPENING BID HAS A DIFFERENT MEANING THAN A DOUBLE OF A SUIT BID. IT SHOWS A HAND AS GOOD AS OR BETTER THAN THE OPENING NT BID. PARTNER SHOULD NORMALLY PASS THE DOUBLE OF 1NT AS THE INTENT IS PENALTY.

REBIDDING AFTER MAKING
A TAKEOUT DOUBLE

When the bidding comes back to you after you have made a takeout double, you will know the approximate size of partner's hand. If he had an opening hand, he would go directly to game. If not, he would bid something less than game and you would have to decide if game is a possibility.

If you have made a takeout double of 1♡ with

    ♠ A 4 3 2
    ♥ 3 2
    ♦ K J 3 2
    ♣ A J 2

and partner responded 1♠, you should pass at your next turn. Partner has at best 8 points and you have 14. There are no more than 22 points between the two hands. Game is out of the question since 26 points are needed; there is no point in taking another bid. Notice that this is a totally different situation than when you have *opened* the bidding and partner has responded with one of a suit.

If you made a takeout double of 1♠ with

    ♠ 3
    ♥ A 9 8 7
    ♦ A 8 7 6
    ♣ K Q 4 3

and partner responded with 2♡, pass. Partner didn't jump; this was the minimum level that he could bid his heart suit. Partner's bid of 2♡ shows 0-8 points.

If you made a takeout double of 1♡ with

    ♠ A 5 4 3
    ♥ 3 2
    ♦ A 8 3 2
    ♣ A K J

and partner responded with 2♠, showing 9-11 points, bid 4♠. You have 17 points in support of spades. Even if partner has only 9 points, there are enough for game.

If you made a takeout double of 1♢ with

    ♠ A 4 3 2
    ♥ A Q 4 2
    ♦ 3 2
    ♣ A 3 2

and partner bids 2♠, there may be a game. You have 15 points in support of spades. If partner has 9, you are short, but if partner has 11, there are enough. Bid 3♠. This invites partner to go on. With 9 points, he should pass; with 11, he should bid game, and with 10 he must make a judgment decision.

WHEN REBIDDING AFTER MAKING A TAKEOUT DOUBLE, ADD YOUR POINTS TO WHAT PARTNER HAS:
■ IF THERE ARE ENOUGH FOR GAME, BID IT.
■ IF THERE ARE NOT ENOUGH POINTS FOR GAME, PASS.
■ IF THERE ARE POSSIBLY ENOUGH POINTS FOR GAME, MAKE AN INVITATIONAL BID.

Anytime you make a takeout double and bid again you show extra values. **Anytime you make a takeout double and bid again you show extra values**—just wanted to make sure you heard that.

An Advanced Point—If partner bids the opponent's suit after a takeout double, it is not because of wanting to play it there; that is not one of his choices. If partner has good cards in the opponent's suit, he would either pass for penalty or bid NT. Therefore, a bid of the opponent's suit after a takeout double has a special meaning. It says that there are enough points for game, but there is a problem in deciding what would be the best game. If partner "cue" bids the opponent's suit, you should cooperate in the search for the best game. Partner may have four hearts and four spades and wants to be sure to play in the 4-4 fit so name a four-card major; presumably you will have at least one.

QUIZ

Indicate whether the double is for takeout or penalty in the following auctions.

	North	East	South	West
1.	1♠	2♡	Dbl	
2.	1♠	pass	2♠	Dbl
3.	1NT	2♡	Dbl	
4.	1♠	pass	2♣	Dbl
5.	2♠	pass	4♠	Dbl
6.	1♠	pass	pass	Dbl

If your RHO opens 1♡, what do you do with the following hands?

7. ♠ A K 4 3 2   8. ♠ A   9. ♠ K 8 6 2
    ♥ 4 3   ♥ K 4 3 2   ♥ 4 3
    ♦ A 3 2   ♦ Q 6 4 2   ♦ A K 4 2
    ♣ Q 6 4   ♣ K 7 6 2   ♣ Q J 2

10. ♠ A J   11. ♠ 8 4 3 2
    ♥ K J 4   ♥ 4
    ♦ A Q 2   ♦ A K 4 3 2
    ♣ J 6 4 3 2   ♣ A J 3

12. Your RHO opened 1♡, you made a takeout double and partner responded 1 ♠. What is your next call with this hand?   ♠ A 4 3 2
                                                                                                                        ♥ 4 3
                                                                                                                        ♦ A J 9
                                                                                                                        ♣ K 6 5 2

13. With the same conditions, what do you do if partner responded 2♠?

14. Your RHO opened 1♡, you made a takeout double and partner responded with 2♣. What is your next call?   ♠ A J 3 2
                                                                                                            ♥ 4 2
                                                                                                            ♦ A K 4 2
                                                                                                            ♣ 9 4 2

15. Your RHO opened 1♦, you doubled and partner bid 2♠. What is your next call with this hand?

    ♠ A Q 4 2
    ♥ K 4 3 2
    ♦ 4 2
    ♣ A J 4

ANSWERS

1. Penalty
2. Takeout
3. Penalty
4. Takeout
5. Penalty
6. Takeout
7. Bid 1♠
8. Pass
9. Double
10. 1NT
11. Double; if the 5-card suit were a major, you should overcall instead.
12. Pass
13. Pass
14. Pass. Another bid would show extra values.
15. Bid 3♠. This invites partner to bid 4 if he is at the top of his bid.

Chapter TEN

NOTRUMP AND THE STAYMAN CONVENTION

26 HCP = game
33 HCP = small slam
37 HCP = grand slam

Review of 1NT opening—A 1 NT opening bid shows a hand of 15, 16, 17 or 18 HCP and is rather balanced, meaning no singletons or voids, and no more than one doubleton. Distribution is never counted when bidding NT.

After your partner has opened 1NT and you, as responder, are pleased to play in NT, you bid as follows:

HCP
0-7   Usually pass. Some exceptions will be shown later.
8-9   The partnership may or may not have the 26 points needed for game in NT. Bid 2NT. This invites the opener to go to game (3NT) if he is in the upper part of his range, 17-18 points.
10-14 Bid 3NT. You want to be in game, no more, no less.
15-16 There is at least a game, possibly a slam. Bid 4NT. Partner will notice that you bid one beyond game. Since it is pointless to be in 4NT when 3NT is game, this asks partner to bid 6NT if he is on top of his bid, 17 or 18, but to pass with 15 or 16.
17-18 Bid 6NT. Your combined points are 32-36. When you are at worst within one point of what you need, bid it.
19-20 You have at least a small slam, possibly a grand. Bid 5NT. This forces at least 6NT and invites a grand slam. If partner is on 15 or 16 he bids 6NT, but with 17 or 18 he bids 7NT.

If partner opens 1NT and you have the following hands, plan your responses.

1. ♠ 4 3 2
   ♥ A 4
   ♦ 8 7 5 2
   ♣ Q 6 5 2

2. ♠ A J 2
   ♥ 3 2
   ♦ K Q J 4
   ♣ 7 5 3 2

3. ♠ A 4
   ♥ 4 3 2
   ♦ 8 6 5 2
   ♣ A 5 4 2

4. ♠ A 4 3   5. ♠ 5 3 2
   ♥ A K J   ♥ A K 2
   ♦ 3 2   ♦ K Q 3 2
   ♣ K Q J 3 2   ♣ K J 4

1. Pass. You have only 6 points, so the partnership has, at best, 24 points (6 + 18) which is not enough for game so there is no point in bidding. Notice that when partner opens with one of a suit, you should bid with 6 points as partner could be on as many as 20+ points and you could miss a game. A 1 NT opening has a maximum of 18 points.

2. Bid 3NT as you are the one who knows that the points are sufficient for game. It should not be of concern to you that you have honors in only two suits. Partner's hand is better than yours, so he almost certainly has cards in the other suits. You have enough points for game and NT likely is the best bet.

3. Bid 2NT. This is a situation in which you can't be sure of game, as you have 8 points. If partner has only 15 or 16, you would not want to be in game, but if partner has 17 or 18, you would have a combined 25 or 26 and game likely would make. This says "we could have game, partner." Opener should pass with 15 or 16, but accept the invitation with 17 or 18.

4. Bid a direct 6NT. This may be a traumatic experience the first time you do it, but the points are there for a small slam. So bid it!

5. You have 16 points, which is clearly enough for game and could be enough for slam. If opener has 15 or 16, game would be high enough, but if opener has 17 or 18, you would want to be in slam. Bid 4NT, one more than necessary for game. This invites partner to go to slam. He will pass with 15 or 16, but bid 6NT with 17 or 18.

THE STAYMAN CONVENTION

Many times, when responding to an opening bid of 1NT, you will have hands with one or two four-card major suits. These are the hands that are difficult to handle with natural bidding. This is why the **Stayman Convention** has remained popular for many years. A "convention" is a bid that shows nothing about the suit bid, but rather asks a question of partner or describes a particular type of hand.

If partner opens 1NT and you have   ♠ A 4 3 2
                           ♥ A Q 3 2
                           ♦ 8 7 4 3
                           ♣ 4

you need to know specifically if partner has either four hearts or four spades. If he does, the major suit would surely be the best contract; if he does not, you'll settle for 3NT.

A response of 2♣ over a 1NT opening is the Stayman Convention. This bid says nothing about clubs, but asks a question of the opener. It asks the opener to name a four-card major if he has one. If opener has a four-card heart suit or a four-card spade suit, he would bid it. With four of each suit, traditionally, spades are shown first. IF OPENER DOESN'T HAVE A FOUR-CARD MAJOR, HE BIDS 2◊. This says nothing about diamonds, but rather says only that the hand does not have four hearts or four spades. If, in the above example, you bid 2♣ and opener rebids 2◊, you should bid 3NT. Opener doesn't have four hearts or four spades, so you can forget about playing in a major suit, as there is no eight-card fit. Also, you can now feel better about the club suit; since partner hasn't many cards in the majors, he is more likely to have the club suit well covered.

The Stayman Convention, used only over NT openers, is primarily used to try to locate 4-4 major suit fits. In general, it shows at least one four-card major and at least 8 points. A couple of unusual uses of Stayman will be mentioned later, but normally you don't use Stayman unless you have at least one four-card major suit and 8 or more HCP.

If partner opens 1NT and you have
♠ Q 6 4 3
♥ 3 2
♦ 4 3 2
♣ A K Q 6

you begin with 2♣. If partner responds 2◊, showing no four-card major, you bid 3NT, as you have enough points for game.

If partner opened 1NT and you had
♠ 8
♥ K 6 4 3
♦ A J 3 2
♣ 8 7 5 2

you would bid 2♣. If partner now bids 2♥, you happily bid 4♥. You have enough for game, since you can count your distribution when you know you are going to be in a trump suit. If partner bids 2◊, showing no four-card major, you next bid 2NT. This shows 8-9 points, just like a direct 1NT—2NT bid, only you stopped first to ask about a major suit. Partner would pass with 15-16 HCP and bid 3NT with 17-18. If partner should bid 2♠ over your 2♣ bid, again, bid 2NT, as partner knows you were interested in a major suit. When you refuse spades, it had to have been hearts that you wanted to hear.

Sometimes, as responder, you have a weak hand, with no interest in game, but you would rather play in a suit than in NT. If, for example, you hold

♠ 7 6 5
♥ J 8 7 6 3 2   (eg., 2♥- **"DROP DEAD" BID**)
♦ 3
♣ 8 3 2

and partner opens 1NT, you can easily see that your hand rates to take no tricks if you pass. Also, your combined point count is 16-19, less than half the deck. Since your hand probably has no entries, your partner would have to play entirely out of his hand, which is a great disadvantage. You would like, therefore, to be able to bid 2♥, and have partner pass, as your hand will take some tricks with hearts as trump. For this reason, bids of 2♦, 2♥ and 2♠, over a 1NT opening, are *known affectionately as **drop-dead bids***, 0-7 HCP with at least five cards of the suit bid (2♣ you will remember is Stayman). It is rare in bridge to take a bid with a very weak hand. In these situations it is done to improve the contract. Opener should, in general, pass the response of 2♦, ♥, or ♠. The only time he should bid again after he has opened 1 NT and you have bid 2♥, for example, is when he has a maximum hand and has a heart fit.

As an example, if you opened 1NT with
♠ K 9 7
♥ K J 8 3
♦ A K 9 8
♣ A 3

and partner bids 2♥, even though partner has shown a weak hand, you really like his heart bid. Bid 3♥, which says "Unless your hand is really sick, bid 4H." If partner has one of these two hands

1. ♠ 4 3   2. ♠ 2
    ♥ Q 6 4 3 2   ♥ Q 7 6 4 3 2
    ♦ 6 4 2   ♦ 5 3
    ♣ 8 6 3   ♣ K 5 4 3

he should pass 3♥ with the first hand and bid 4♥ with the second.

Many game-going hands with a long minor suit are better off played in NT, since it is often easier to take nine tricks in NT than 11 tricks in clubs or diamonds. If partner opens 1NT and you have

♠ Q J
♥ 6 5 4
♦ A K 4 3 2
♣ 8 7 5

bid 3NT as that will make more often than 5◊ even if partner has good diamonds.

However, if it can be determined that the partnership owns eight or more cards of a major suit, that is usually a safer contract. If you have

♠ 4 3
♥ A J 6 4 3
♦ A J 5
♣ 6 4 3

and partner opens 1NT, you know you have enough points for game. If partner has three or more hearts, you would want to be in 4♡, but if partner has a doubleton heart, you would want to be in 3NT. People often make the mistake of bidding Stayman, which asks the wrong question; because partner will tell you if he has a four-card major, and you are looking for 3 hearts. You can't bid 2♡ as that is a drop dead bid. Solution: Bid 3♡, which says that you want to be at least in game (10+ HCP) and that you have a five-card heart suit. Usually you will have exactly five cards, although it could be more. Partner should raise you to 4♡ with three or more hearts, and bid 3NT with a doubleton heart.

If partner opens 1NT and you have

♠ A J 8 6 5 3
♥ K 6 4
♦ 6 5 3
♣ 4

bid 4♠. You know there are at least eight spades between the hands, as partner must have at least two. You have 8 HCP plus a six-card spade suit, and a singleton. The 4♠ bid shows no interest whatsoever in slam.

If partner opens 1 NT, you would also use Stayman with this hand.

♠ A 5 4 3
♥ A 7 6 4 2
♦ Q 4 3
♣ 3

Although you have a five-card suit, you don't want to bid 3♡, because if partner bids 3NT, you would then have no way to know if he has four spades in his hand. Start this hand with 2♣. If partner bids 2♡ or 2♠, you will raise either to game. If partner bids 2◇, you jump to 3♡, which is forcing just as a direct jump to 3♡ would be. Partner will raise to 4♡ with three hearts and bid 3NT with a doubleton heart. You now have checked out both majors before deciding where to play this hand. **With a five-card major and a four-card major, start with Stayman.**

If, as opener, you bid 1NT with

♠ A K 4 2
♥ A 5 4 2
♦ A 3 2
♣ Q 2

and partner bids 2♣, you would bid 2♠. If partner now bids 3NT, you should bid 4♡. Partner has expressed an interest in playing this hand in a major suit. If he doesn't have four spades, he must have four hearts.

The following are more unusual uses of Stayman. Be sure the above information is understood thoroughly before reading on.

Although Stayman is primarily used to locate 4-4 fits and with 8 or more points, there are some exceptions. Suppose your partner opens 1 NT and you have

♠ J 7 6 4
♥ 7 6 5 3
♦ 8 7 6 4 2
♣ — — —

You could improve your chances of a plus score if you could play this in one of your suits. Bid 2♣. Partner will, of course, think you have 8 + points, but that's okay. He will soon find out what you are doing, because when he bids 2◇, 2♡ or 2♠, you pass. Remember when responding to Stayman, those are his only choices. He either has a four-card major and bids it, or says he doesn't have one by bidding 2◇.

If partner opens 1NT and you have

♠ A 10 4 3 2
♥ K 3 2
♦ J 3 2
♣ 4 2

your hand is too good to respond 2♠ (0-7 HCP) and not good enough for 3♠ (10+ HCP). This is one of the few exceptions when you use Stayman with a five-card major suit. You bid 2♣. If partner bids 2♠, you raise to 4♠, but if partner bids 2◊ or 2♡, you bid 2♠. This shows exactly five spades and 8-9 HCP.

If your partner opens 1NT and you have a bad hand with long clubs, my best advice is to pass. 2♣ is for Stayman. For now, live without a drop dead in clubs. If your partner opens 1NT and you have a bad hand with long clubs, pass, put your hand on the table and leave the room.

If partner were to open 2NT (22-24), 3♣ is Stayman. Partner's hand is so big, only 3 points are needed for game; therefore this is also enough to use Stayman. It is a simple arithmetic question as to how many points you need to bid over various NT bids. For example, if a pair were playing their opening 2NT range a little bit lower, responder would need a little more.

AFTER A NOTRUMP OPENING RESPONDER IS CAPTAIN.

Your partner has opened 1NT. What is your first response with the following hands?

1. ♠ K 9 7 5 3 2 ♥ 9 7 5 ◊ 3 2 ♣ 6 5	2. ♠ K 9 8 6 ♥ 4 ◊ K 5 4 2 ♣ 10 9 5 4	3. ♠ A J 9 8 4 ♥ 4 3 ◊ Q J 9 2 ♣ K 8
4. ♠ 7 4 ♥ Q J 10 7 6 5 ◊ 3 ♣ K J 4 2	5. ♠ A Q 9 7 5 ♥ K J 6 4 2 ◊ 9 3 ♣ 5	6. ♠ 9 2 ♥ Q 8 5 ◊ K Q 5 4 3 ♣ K 9 3
7. ♠ Q 9 7 6 ♥ 3 ◊ A K 6 4 ♣ 8 7 4 2	8. ♠ 8 7 ♥ A K 10 5 3 ◊ K Q 4 ♣ 10 8 4	9. ♠ A 3 ♥ K 4 2 ◊ K Q 9 7 5 ♣ K 7 5
10. ♠ 9 5 ♥ K J 8 7 6 5 ◊ A 4 2 ♣ 10 2	11. ♠ A Q 7 5 ♥ A J 10 8 ◊ 4 ♣ A 4 3 2	12. ♠ A 10 8 6 ♥ Q 7 6 5 4 ◊ A 9 7 6 ♣ — — —

ANSWERS

1. 2♠
2. Pass
3. 3♠
4. 4♡
5. 3♠—if partner bids 3NT, your next bid will be 4♡.
6. 3NT
7. 2♣
8. 3♡
9. 4NT
10. 4♡
11. 2♣
12. 2♣—if partner bids 2◊, you next bid 3♡.

Chapter ELEVEN
PREEMPTIVE BIDDING

A preemptive opening bid is a bid of three or more of a suit and is designed to interrupt the opponents' efforts to accurately bid to their best contract. It is made with a long good suit and very little strength outside that suit. The hand has fewer than 10 points in high cards. It is the modern style to have no aces and typically no kings outside of the suit. Your values should be in your suit, and little or nothing outside the suit.

Suppose the opponents are **vulnerable,** you are **not vulnerable,** and as dealer you have

♠ K Q J 9 7 5 3
♥ 4 3
♦ 8
♣ 7 5 2

An opening 3♠ bid might rate to be a very useful preempt. The reasoning is this: You have six tricks with spades as trumps; if partner has two tricks for you, such as the AK of clubs, you would only go down one trick; the opponents probably have a game. Your hand rates to take no tricks on defense, as one of the opponents is likely to be short in spades. If partner's hand happens to be weak, and you are doubled, you may lose 500 points, but then the opponents surely have a game, which will give them 700 bonus points plus their trick score. They could even have a slam, which is certainly harder for them to find when they have to start bidding at such a high level. When you preempt, if partner is on the weak side, the opponents may fail to bid the game they have coming or bid a wrong game. Sometimes partner has a big hand and the opponents enter your auction, and partner doubles and beats them a bunch. (Vulnerable doubled down three is 800 points.) There are many strange results when the bidding starts so high.

It is a problem for a person with

♠ 6 4 3
♥ A 8 6 4 3 2
♦ A Q
♣ K Q

to know what to do when the person in front of him opens 3♠. This is the real bonus of preempting. It's not only that you may save points on the scoring if they miss their game, but they may bid an impossible game or slam or a wrong one when forced to make a decision at a high level.

Because of the fact that it's rather fun to be the cause of the opponents going wrong, the whole world seems to love to preempt. There's a bit of larceny in all of us. One of the bad things that could happen if you get too carried away with preempting is that your partner would not know what to expect. Partner could happen to be the person with the big hand. For this reason, some guidelines are needed to establish what makes for effective preempts. The traditional way of thinking for years was the rule of 2 or 3. That meant that not vulnerable you could afford to have six winners in the trump suit and vulnerable you would need seven tricks. Although that is not bad advice, the current trend is to be looser. In this text we are going to relax a little on the rule of 2 or 3.

The first hand at the beginning of this chapter is the classic preempt for nonvulnerable. Most players today wouldn't bat an eye at bidding 3♡ with that hand if both sides were vulnerable. Many players preempt with as little as KJ86432 in the suit, if not vulnerable, and that is okay. Vulnerable, preempting with that suit is not a good idea as it could be very dangerous. It is important that you and your partner agree on your style of preempting. The lighter style could be expressed that not vulnerable you have *roughly* 6 tricks, and vulnerable you have 6 to 7. Even if you like the lighter or at least possibly a little less for your preempts, you don't want to go totally berserk. A good recommendation is that vulnerable you are always a little careful; and not vulnerable against vulnerable you might be a little frisky.

You must consider the consequences if you get doubled. Even with a little flexibility, your preempt in first or second seat should be:

A GOOD SUIT OF SEVEN CARDS WITH A MINIMUM OF TWO HONORS, VERY LITTLE STRENGTH OUTSIDE OF THE SUIT AND NOT STRONG ENOUGH TO OPEN WITH ONE OF A SUIT.

It is especially important to stick to your agreements when partner is not a passed hand. He might have a good hand and needs to be able to rely on you for what you said you have. It isn't good to have decidedly more or decidedly less than expected.

In third seat it's okay to be more flexible, even having a pretty good hand, because partner has passed so you won't be likely to lead him astray when he is known to have less than an opener.

ONE PROBLEM with preempting is that many partners tend to bid too much after you preempt, such as bidding game with just an opening hand, and that doesn't work well at all. Later in this chapter is a discussion on responding after your partner preempts.

No one is vulnerable and you are dealer with the following hands. What do you do?

1. ♠ A 7 6 5 4 3 2   2. ♠ 4   3. ♠ A Q 8 7 5 4 2
   ♥ K 5 4   ♥ K Q J 7 6 5 2   ♥ A 5
   ♦ 7 6   ♦ 8 7 5   ♦ 6 5 3
   ♣ 3   ♣ 7 4   ♣ 9

1. Pass. Your suit isn't good enough for a preemptive bid; you also have an outside K. Very likely, you will have a chance to bid your spades later. The problem with preempting with hands that have defensive tricks is that, although you may have "stolen the bid," it may be of no value because the opponents can't make anything.
2. This is a classic 3♡ preempt.
3. This hand is too good to preempt. Although you have only 10 HCP points, your suit is good and with your outside ace you should open this hand 1♠. If you had never heard of preempts you would have opened this hand 1♠ and would have been right. People often get carried away with seven-card suits and preempt for all the wrong reasons.

The second important consideration in preempting is vulnerability. There are four conditions:
1. They are vulnerable—you are not. Ideal time to preempt.
2. No one is vulnerable. Fairly good conditions for a preempt.
3. Everyone is vulnerable. OK time, but remember that you are vulnerable
4. You are vulnerable—they are not. This is an uninspired time to preempt. You should have a good reason—highly distributional, maybe an 8th card, or a belief that a little torture builds character.

It is possible to preempt with a bid of four of a suit as well as a bid on the three level. Always be aware of vulnerability, so you know how much you are risking.

Four-level bids occur less often as you usually will have eight+ cards for this bid. The same general conditions apply, i. e., good suit and little outside; however, when you open 4♡ or 4♠ you are in game so you have a little more latitude. An outside ace is okay, but not much more. An outside AK would be too much, because you could easily miss a slam. Partner will not expect you to have that much. With a good long suit and outside cards open with one of a suit.

With neither side vulnerable, you have   ♠   A   K   J   7   6   5   3   2
                                         ♥   7   6   3
                                           ♦   4   3
                                           ♣   —   —   —

Open 4♠. You have a probable eight tricks in your own hand with spades as trump, so doubled you would be down two, or 300 points. It may cause the opponents to miss something or drive them into a contract that fails where another one easily would have made. You are putting pressure on your opponents, but because your suit is good, your own neck is not on the chopping block.

- **Once you have preempted, you have told your story. You should not bid again unless your partner forces you.**
- If partner is an unpassed hand, a new suit below the game level is forcing.
- After three passes, there is little merit in a preempt of the usual sort, as the opponents have had a chance to bid and didn't.

When partner preempts, pass with most opening hands or even a few extra points. You need to have enough quick tricks or quick winners to make a game.

> QUICK TRICKS ARE TRICKS THAT YOU EXPECT TO
> TAKE THE FIRST OR SECOND TIME THE SUIT IS LED.

A	=	1
AK	=	2
AKQ	=	2 (first or second time suit led)
KQ	=	1
AQ	=	1½
K2	=	½

When partner has preempted, you need a minimum of 3½ quick tricks to bid game in a major suit. Let's take a classic nonvulnerable preempt by partner. Partner has opened 3♡ with

♠ 3 2
♥ K Q J 7 6 4 2
♦ J 7
♣ 6 5

and you have:

1. ♠ K Q J 7 2
    ♥ 9 8
    ♦ K Q 2
    ♣ Q J 3

2. ♠ A 6 5 4
    ♥ 8 5
    ♦ A 4
    ♣ A K 7 3 2

1. Pass. You have an opening hand, but only 2 quick tricks. Partner can't be expected to take more than 6 tricks. You need 3½ quick tricks to bid 4♡.
2. Bid 4♡. You have 4 quick tricks. It seems funny raising partner with only two cards, but when partner has announced a seven-card suit, two in your hand is good support. With enough quick tricks, a singleton in partner's suit would be adequate.

QUIZ

1. A preemptive bid on the three level should have ___ cards of the suit.
2. The most advantageous time to preempt is when the opponents are ___ and you are ___.
3. In responding to a preempt, ___ are the important considerations.
4. AK is ___ quick trick(s).
5. AQ is ___ quick trick(s).
6. KQ is ___ quick trick(s).
7. K32 is ___ quick trick(s).
8. AJ2 is ___ quick trick(s).

With both sides not vulnerable, your RHO has passed. What do you bid?

9. ♠ K Q 10 8 7 3 2
    ♥ 9 7 4
    ♦ 5 4
    ♣ 5

10. ♠ A Q 7 6 4 3 2
    ♥ K Q 3
    ♦ 4 3
    ♣ 5

11. ♠ J 9 8 7 5 3 2
    ♥ A K 2
    ♦ 7 5
    ♣ 2

Your *partner* opens 3♡, the next person passes. You are *responder*.

12. ♠ K Q J 7 6 5 2   13. ♠ A K 3
    ♥ 6   ♥ 6 5
    ♦ J 10 2   ♦ A 7 6 5
    ♣ 5 4   ♣ K Q 4 3

ANSWERS

1. 7
2. Vulnerable, nonvulnerable
3. Quick tricks
4. 2
5. 1¹/₂
6. 1
7. ¹/₂
8. 1
9. Bid 3♠. You aren't vulnerable
10. Bid 1♠. This is much too good to preempt.
11. Pass. Your suit is bad and you have too much outside.
12. Pass. If you even *think* of bidding, you have made an error.
    (A new suit would show a very strong hand and would be forcing.)
13. Bid 4♡. You have 4 quick tricks.

Chapter TWELVE
SLAM BIDDING

The two most important aspects of slam bidding are:

1. Knowing that there are enough points for slam (or enough tricks with distributional hands where tricks can be counted).
2. Knowing that the opponents can't take the first two tricks.

The person who should pursue a slam is the person who knows that the points or tricks are there. This may or may not be the person with the bigger hand. (33 points will usually yield a small slam and 37 points a grand slam.)

Partner opens 1◇ and you have
- ♠ K Q 10 2
- ♥ A 5 4 3 2
- ♦ K 3 2
- ♣ 6

You bid 1♡ and partner next bids 2♠, your good four-card suit. Partner has made a jump shift showing 19+ points. You know that you have a place to play (spades) and that the partnership has enough points for slam, as you have 12 high, plus a singleton, which is worth 2 points when you have found a trump fit. It is up to you to pursue the slam.

> ### The one who knows goes

Next you pick up
- ♠ A 5 3
- ♥ A Q J 7 5
- ♦ A Q 5 4
- ♣ 7

and open 1♡. Partner bids 3♡ (13-16 points). Your hand has 17 high and 2 for the singleton plus two perks—A good five-card suit, and 4 quick tricks. It is up to you to take action.

If partner opens 2NT (22-24 balanced) and you have
- ♠ A 4 3 2
- ♥ K J 4
- ♦ Q J 5 4
- ♣ 4 3

you are the one who knows that there are 33+ points. Bid 6NT.

(If you play weak two-bids, you have more notrump bids available because of the strong and artificial 2♣. Partner would show the hand of about 23 HCP as follows: 2♣ opening, 2◇ response, and a rebid of 2NT.)

By the time you read this chapter, you have probably played Blackwood for a quite a while, but the bid is sometime misused so the information may be helpful. It is possible to have enough points for slam, but be missing controls. In suit bidding, asking for aces to make sure that the opponents do not have two aces usually is necessary and using Blackwood is the standard way of asking for aces. When a partnership has been bidding suits and there is slam interest, when one or the other bids 4NT, as in the auction 1♠—3♠—4NT, 4NT asks how many aces partner has. Partner answers alphabetically.

5 ♣	=	0 aces (or all 4)
5 ♦	=	1 ace
5 ♥	=	2 aces
5 ♠	=	3 aces

> The purpose of Blackwood is to make sure you have at least 3 aces.

If you have asked for aces and have found that you have all of them, you can check for kings by bidding 5NT. 5NT promises all 4 aces and is used only when interested in a grand slam.

6 ♣	=	0 kings (or all 4)
6 ♦	=	1 king
6 ♥	=	2 kings
6 ♠	=	3 kings

If you open 1 ♠ with ♠ A K 6 5 4
                               ♥ K Q J 6
                               ♦ K J 3
                               ♣ 7

and partner bids 3♠ (13-16 points), you have 17 high and 2 for the singleton plus a couple of perks- a good five-card suit and honors together (as in the heart suit). You are ready to go to slam, but you want to be sure that partner has at least two aces. Bid 4NT. If partner replies 5◇, return to 5♠ as you are missing two aces. But if partner bids 5♡ or 5♠, bid 6♠.

Blackwood is a useful convention when properly applied. First, it should be clear that the points (or tricks) are sufficient for slam, and second, you need some assurance that the opponents cannot take the first two tricks. Blackwood does not apply directly over an opening bid of 1NT or 2NT, because slams in NT are made on high-card strength. The opponents can't have two aces if you and your partner have 33 HCP.

If you use Blackwood and the information you receive from partner is not useful to you, you asked the wrong question; meaning Blackwood should not have been used. Suppose there have been two passes and you open 1♠ in third chair with

♠ A K 8 7 5 4 3
♥ A K Q 4
♦ 6 5
♣ — — —

and partner bids 3♠. As a passed hand he is showing about 11 points counting everything. For your information, if partner passed originally and he has a hand that grew to 13 points, when you opened 1S, he has to take it upon himself to bid game. Having heard partner pass, you will not picture him having an opening hand.

Back to this hand—partner has about 11 points. The tricks are there for slam interest. Notice, with long, strong suits we can count tricks, which is more effective than counting points. With partner raising spades, you have 10 or more trumps, so

- no trump losers
- no heart losers quite certainly, because if partner is short, you can trump the small one in dummy, and if partner is long, the A, K, & Q should gather up all of the opponents' hearts
- no club losers.

If you bid 4NT and partner has one ace, you don't know what to do. If you knew that it was the ace of diamonds, you would be assured that the opponents couldn't take the first two tricks. If, however, partner's ace was in clubs, the opponents might be able to cash the first two diamonds right off the top. When you need to know which ace partner has, cue bidding is very effective.

Cue bidding is somewhat involved so it works best in a regular partnership. Once a major suit has been picked, that suit is going to be trump. When the suit is "set" such as 1♡ (Pass) 3♡, any new suit bid past 3 of our major suit must have some special meaning, because we can't stop short of game when we are already past 3 of our suit. A bid of a new suit higher than 3♡ should be a cue bid, looking for slam. The cue bid shows first-round control, most commonly an ace, but it could be a void.

With the last hand, after (1♠—3♠) bid 4♣, which says that you have first-round control of clubs. 4♣ is the cheapest suit you can cue-bid. With more than one ace or first-round control to cue-bid, you always cue-bid the cheapest one first. If your partner now bids 4♠, that is not a cue bid; he is returning to the trump suit because he has no aces to cue-bid. At this point you should make another effort to reach slam by cue bidding 5♡; you are showing the ace of hearts and are saying to partner that you are worried about diamonds. That should be obvious because both of the other suits have been cue-bid and you went to 5♡ knowing partner didn't have the ace of diamonds. At this point you will happily settle for second-round control. If your partner has something like KQ54 of diamonds, or a singleton diamond, he should rise to the occasion and bid 6♠.

South (you)	North
♠ A 4 3	♠ K Q 9
♥ A K Q 6 5	♥ J 10 8 7
♦ 7 5	♦ K Q 3
♣ K Q 2	♣ A 8 7

Another example. You open the South hand with 1♡ and partner raises to 3♡. Your hand is worth 19 points plus a perk for the good five-card heart suit. For your information, anytime you have 19 counting everything and partner has shown 13+ you should pursue a slam.

The generalization is:
When you are within one point of your desired goal or better, go for it. So with 32 or more we try for a slam, and with 25 or more we bid a game. Concerning aces, Blackwood may not give you the information you need. If partner has only one ace, you might be off two diamond tricks. An accurate way to bid these hands would be

	South	North
	1♥	3♥
(1)	3♠	4♣ (2)
(3)	4♥	6♥ (4)

(1) A cue bid of the ace of spades

(2) A cue bid of the ace of clubs

(3) A return to the agreed-upon trump suit, denying the ace of diamonds. This is not a cue bid of the ace of hearts. The trump ace can never be cue-bid. If you need to know about the ace of trumps, the only way to find that out is by using Blackwood. Now put yourself in the North position.

(4) Partner has announced that points are there for slam. Both clubs and spades have been cue-bid; partner is obviously worried about diamonds. He has denied having the ace and you are looking at the KQ. You know that the opponents can't take the first two tricks in diamonds. Partner presumably has good hearts. He wouldn't likely be trying for a slam with bad diamonds if he didn't have good trumps.

There are a few other points of slam bidding that you will want to know as you become more experienced. Minor suits can be a problem in slam bidding. Suppose you and your partner have agreed on clubs as the trump suit, as in the auction 1♣—3♣ and you know that there are enough points for slam. Suppose you bid 4NT with only one ace in your hand and partner answers with 5◇, showing one ace. It's too late for you to stop in 5♣. You might want to try 5NT as your only chance for a makeable contract, but if you bid that, partner will answer kings. A new suit by you, at this point, such as 5♡ or 5♠ requests partner to bid 5NT, which you will pass. Remember, clubs were agreed upon as trumps, so a new suit on the five level can't be for play.

Another situation you can face is the following: partner opened 1♠ and you bid 3♠ with

    ♠   J 10 5 3   2

    ♥   — — —

    ◆ K Q 8 2

    ♣ A 5 4 2

If partner now bids 4NT, you have a problem. You don't like to answer 5◇ as you have control of hearts as well as your ace, but if you answer 5♡ showing two aces, partner may get overzealous and go for a grand slam because he thought you had two aces. (He may have a good heart suit, and thinking you have the ace, he could count 13 tricks.) The best solution is to jump to six in your void (6♡) which shows one ace and a void in the suit in which you jumped. Partner will now bid 6♠ unless the heart void would be what he needed to bid 7♠. Be sure you don't jump in a void which is higher-ranking than the agreed-upon suit. If hearts were the suit agreed upon and partner bid 4NT, when you have 1 ace and a void in spades, a 6♠ bid by you would force partner to bid 7♡. In this situation, you respond to partner's 4NT bid with a bid of 6♡. This says that you have one ace and a void in a higher-ranking suit, which in this case would have to be spades.

If you should have no aces and a void, it's usually best to simply show no aces (5♣). If you should happen to have two aces and a void, a grand slam should be a consideration if the hands appear to fit well.

QUIZ

1.   ____ points will usually produce a small slam.
2.   ____ points will usually produce a grand slam.
3.   If you bid Blackwood, a response of 5♡ shows ____ ace(s), 5♣ shows ____ ace(s), 5 ♠ shows ____ ace(s) and 5◇ shows ____ ace(s).
4.   In the auction 1♡—3♡—4NT—5◇—5NT, what does 5NT mean?
5.   South opens the auction with 1♡, North bids 3♡ and South then bids 4♣.
      - What does 4♣ mean?
      - Can the South hand have the ace of spades?
      - Can the South hand have the ace of diamonds?
6.   In the auction 1♡—2♠—3♠—4NT—6◇, what does 6◇ mean?
7.   In the auction 1NT—4NT, is 4NT Blackwood?
8.   In the auction 2♡—3♡—4NT—6♡, what does 6♡ mean?
9.   In the auction 1♠—3♠—4♣—4♠, what does 4♣ mean? What does 4♠ mean?
10.   In the auction 1♣—3♣—4NT—5♡, what does 5♡ mean?

ANSWERS

1. 33
2. 37
3. 2, 0 (or 4), 3, 1
4. It asks for kings and promises all the aces.
5. It shows the ace of clubs. No, 3♠ would have been the cheapest cue bid. Yes, he can have the ace of diamonds.

6. One ace and a void in diamonds.
7. No.
8. It shows one ace and a void in spades.
9. It shows the ace of clubs. The hand has no aces to cue-bid.
10. It shows two aces.

Chapter THIRTEEN
WHEN THE OPPONENTS COMPETE WITH AN OVERCALL

This chapter will be limited to one of the most important aspects of how the opponents' bidding affects you, specifically in the situation in which partner has opened, there is an overcall and you are the responder in third seat. This is important because it occurs often.

Is your guess that the interference of an overcall usually hurts you? Most people would answer yes, but the fact is it can:

a. Have no effect on you
b. Get in your way and make life harder
c. Help you

Starting with a common example, you have

♠ A 5 4
♥ 7 5 3
♦ 9 2
♣ J 9 6 4 3

Your partner deals and opens 1♡, followed by the opponent overcalling 2♢. How does this affect you as far as your minimum values for a 2♡ raise? Answer—NOT AT ALL. When you have a scrawny six count with which you would have barely eked out 2♡ without interference, eke it out now also. Some question whether it should show more since you don't have to bid. You don't have to bid if the opponent passes nor do you have to bid now, but it is an opportunity. Don't create a problem for yourself when none exists. This is no doubt your last opportunity at a low level to say that you have support and 6-plus points. Use it.

The maximum points for the 2♡ bid is actually a more interesting question.

First, let's examine the 2♡ raise without interference, showing 6-10 playing points, meaning distribution is counted. Some question if 10 points is too much. Not unless the 10 has some extra perks that make it seem better.

After partner opens 1♡, look at the next three hands. With the first hand

Hand #1   ♠ Q 6 4 3
           ♥ A 9 6
           ♦ 8 5
           ♣ Q J 6 2

most seasoned bridge players would bid 2♡ without a second thought, even though they may have ways to show a hand that is just a bit better. This hand has no perks so there is no reason to stretch. A simple 2♡ bid is good.

So what are easy-to-spot perks? A 4th trump, for example, giving you nine trumps is clearly a perk, so much so that counting it as an extra point is very reasonable. A good side suit is also a perk, the club suit in hand 2 and the spade suit in hand 3.

Hand #2   ♠ 5 4
           ♥ 8 7 5 4
           ♦ A 9 5
           ♣ A J 10 4

Hand #3   ♠ A K 10 4
           ♥ Q 9 4
           ♦ 7 6
           ♣ 9 8 6 5

Both hands 2 & 3 are good enough hands that the perks make them seem more like 11 and can be bid as stronger hands. With hand 2 you could bid 2♣; and say partner bids 2◇—you now bid 2♡. If partner rebids 2NT, instead of 2◇, you next bid 3♡. You are a point short for bidding 2♣, but you are planning ahead here, and when you next go back to hearts, you show about 11 points. This is one way to show a hand a bit too big for 2♡.

With hand #3, you would bid 1♠ and if partner next bids 2♣ or 2◇, you bid 3♡, showing a hand of about 11 playing points (very good 10, 11 or a bad 12). Notice you need to bid 3♡ here—a delayed jump—because the 1♠ bid shows only 6+ points, whereas, in hand two, the 2♣ announces 10+ points, so a delayed jump isn't needed in #2.

Back to interference. Again 1♡, 2◇ overcall, 3♡, by you. What should the 3♡ bid show? Even if you normally play 3♡ as a forcing bid, with interference there is usually not room for changing suits and later coming back to partner's suit without getting too high. Therefore, the recommendation is 1♡, (1♠, 2♣, or 2◇ overcall) 3♡ shows the 11ish point hand (again good 10 to a bad 12).

If an opponent overcalls with a more space-consuming bid such as after partner opens 1♡, the opponent jumps to 2♠, 3♣ or 3◇, responder has a new problem. Suppose you are responder and have a hand where you have a nice 2♡ bid, but now the level is at three. The recommendation is that the 3♡ bid shows about 8-11 pts. With a major-suit fit and some values, it is important that we try to show that if possible. There is no name for this bid. It is simply that when we have a fit and the opponents are in our auction, we sometimes have to alter our ranges a little. After a 1♡ by partner and a 2♠ overcall, bid 3♡ with the following hand.

```
♠  7  6  5
♥  K  6  4  3
♦  A  8  7  5
♣  6  4
```

Passing would feel uncomfortable and bidding 3♡ might make you feel you've stretched—"Sorry partner, I cheated a little." Again, the recommended range for the 3♡ bid is about 8-11 points including distribution and any perks you may find. You are now absolved from guilt and you can cut the disgusting apology.

	Partner	Opponent	You
To sum up:	1♡	2◇ (overcall)	3♡ = 10+ to 12- (11ish)
	1♡	3◇ (overcall)	3♡ = 8 – 11

Same auction: 1♡ (2◇), you are in third seat and you have an opening hand. You will have to make it your job to get to game. You can bid 4♡ directly, or if you have a sound opening hand with support for partner's suit and your partnership is a bit more sophisticated, you can cue-bid 3◇, which shows heart support and a sound opening hand. The bid says nothing at all about your holding in the suit you cue-bid ($\diamond$). The reason for the distinction is in case partner has a strong hand he will know when to consider slam. By having the cue bid available we can distinguish between a distributional hand with which you want to give game a shot and a sound opening hand with trump support. If you have these methods available, the direct $4\heartsuit$ bid could be the same as it would be without interference, the magic-type hand

♠ 6 5 4 3
♥ K 8 7 6 3
♦ 4
♣ Q J 10

and the $3\diamond$ cue bid is the sound opening hand with trump support.

How about this simple little one-level overcall? Partner opens $1\heartsuit$ and the next hand overcalls $1\spadesuit$, and you in third seat hold

♠ 5 4 3 2
♥ K 2
♦ 9 7 5 3
♣ K Q 2

You seem to have no bid. 1NT may cross your mind, but the one thing you promise when the opponents overcall and you bid notrump is at least one honor, usually two, in their suit. If partner had previously bid notrump then you don't need that promise. The immediate 1NT shows at least one spade stopper and 8-10 points. Although you pass now with this hand, the good news is that if partner has a good hand he will bid again at his next turn, and if so you can probably find something meaningful to do next time around. Suppose he bids $2\heartsuit$ at his next turn, showing six cards; you can now raise him to $3\heartsuit$, showing a hand with which you wanted to bid, but only had two hearts.

New situation. Your partner opens $1\spadesuit$ and an opponent overcalls $2\heartsuit$ and you in third seat have a hand with which you are thinking about bidding $3\diamond$. Notice this could be any auction in which bidding your suit takes you to the three level:

1♣ (2♠ jump overcall)
1♡ (3♣ jump overcall)
1♠ (2♡ overcall)

What kind of a hand should you have when you bid a new suit at the three level? Or, more to the point, what kind of hand will partner expect from you? It is forcing, of course, as it is a new suit by responder. The problem with bidding a new suit at that high a level is that you are usually going to get too high, probably game level, whether you planned to or not. Say you bid 3◇ and your partner has a couple of honors in the overcalled suit; he will bid 3NT and you are in game. If he raises your diamonds (4◇) you are at a high level now also. If your hand isn't strong you may be way too high.

Consequently, responder (3rd hand) when bidding a new suit at the three level should show an opening hand or close, because the bid is forcing and you will usually catapult your side into game whether you planned it or not.

On the next hand your partner opens 1♣ and your RHO makes a jump overcall of 2♠. You have

♠ A Q 2
♥ 5 2
♦ K Q J 4 3
♣ 6 4 3

What do you bid? Notice how easily three diamonds can fall out of your mouth before you think of what will happen next. You know partner has no spade honors because they were bid on your right and you have two good honors. If partner bids 4♣ or 4◇ you are now likely to be past your best game, which is probably 3NT. Try to see this coming and bid 3NT right off the bat. If you are concerned about not having hearts stopped, you worry too much.

Partner opens 1♠ and RHO bids 2♡. You have

♠ 7
♥ K J 9 6
♦ J 10 9 5 4
♣ K Q 7

If you were to defend 2♡, you are heavily slated to take three heart tricks because you are over the heart bidder, plus you have a good shot at two club winners. You are also short in partner's spade suit, which means his spade honors should cash. You have the 2♡ bidder booked in your own hand and partner, with an opening hand, should have at least two to three defensive tricks. If you double you should expect to defeat a contract of 2♡ two to three tricks—500 to 800 points if they are vulnerable and 300 to 500 points if they are not. Playing very standard methods with no special conventions (i.e., negative doubles) you are going to get around 500 points in a situation when you would have only a part score if you got the contract. "Double" you say, trying not to raise your voice or climb upon a piece of furniture.

Most players who play mostly social bridge at home with friends and neighbors are wise not to play many conventions, although Blackwood and Stayman are standard tools that are important to know. If your partner is experienced, it should be assumed that he plays these.

For those who play a lot of competitive bridge, negative doubles should be high on the list of conventions to add. Look at the back of this book to see *NEGATIVE DOUBLES,* Volume VIII of the BRIDGE Mini Series.

Chapter FOURTEEN
WHEN THE OPPONENTS COMPETE WITH A TAKEOUT DOUBLE, A 1NT OVERCALL, OR THE UNUSUAL 2NT

Your partner opens 1◇, an opponent makes a takeout double and you are in third chair. There are a number of actions you can take: bid a new suit, raise partner's suit, bid NT, or redouble.

It once was the style of bidding that all good hands of 10 or more HCP started out with a redouble, so with that as the guideline, a new suit bid was by definition fewer than 10 HCP. This is explained only because you may encounter people playing that style. The ***more recent style,*** for a fair amount of years actually, is that a new suit by the responder at the **one** level is forcing—much like the double had never occurred. Therefore the auction 1◇ (double) 1♡ is not limiting the hand to under 10 points. Rather the redouble is saved for certain types of hands (to be discussed shortly) and the new suit at the one level (1♡) could be 6 points or could easily be 13 or more since it is forcing. The current style is much more flexible in that if you want to bid your hand naturally you may do so and be free of the idea that you must redouble with 10+. Rather, you ***may*** redouble with 10 or more; not that you must. This carries with it the awareness that in an auction such as

You	Opponent	Partner	Opponent
1♣	Double	1♠	Pass
2♣	Pass	2◇	

the 2◇ bid would also be forcing because we are playing this auction as if the double hadn't occurred. It is commonplace these days to play 1♠ as forcing in the above auction, but some miss the inference that 2◇ (a new suit by responder) is also forcing. That is the whole point—to be able to show your hand naturally, when you choose to do so.

A new suit at the two level, 1♠ (Double) 2◇, is played as fewer than 10 HCP. The 2◇ bid shows a good six-card suit (or a very good five-card suit), and is not forcing.

The redouble primarily is saved for hands not only with 10+ HCP, but hands with which you have interest in doubling the opponents' final contract. With both sides vulnerable, your partner opens 1♠, double by the opponent, and you have one of the two following hands:

1. ♠ 2
   ♥ A Q 9 2
   ◆ Q 10 9 4
   ♣ K 10 8 7

2. ♠ 7 2
   ♥ A Q 10 3
   ◆ 5 3
   ♣ A 9 8 4 3

After you redouble, partner is expected to either pass or double their bid with all hands except the rare, extremely distributional hands.

1. This is the classic hand with which you want to say "redouble." If LHO bids 2♣, 2◇ or 2♥, partner will no doubt pass and you will double whichever two-level bid they choose. A hefty 500 points is expected to be bestowed upon you, 200 if you are unlucky, and 800 if things go your way.
2. Here you would like to sink your teeth into either 2♣ or 2♥, by doubling the opponents, and if they choose to bid 2◇ partner may have four of those and be able to double that contract. Another bright picture for your side.

If you haven't had much experience doubling the opponents at a low level for profit, the hand below is a good example. Look carefully at the following hand.

North
♠ A K Q 7 4
♥ 2
♦ K Q 7 4
♣ 6 5 4

West
♠ J 10 8 5
♥ 9 8 5 4
♦ 10 3 2
♣ J 10

East
♠ 6 2
♥ K J 6 3
♦ A J 9 6
♣ K Q 7

South (you)
♠ 9 3
♥ A Q 10 7
♦ 8 5
♣ A 9 8 3 2

Partner, North, opens 1♠ and East doubles. You redouble and West doesn't have to bid when there has been a bid by the 3rd hand. The opponents should at some point get to 2♡, their only suit with 8 cards. The defense should do no worse than take 2 spades, 3 hearts, 1 diamond, and 1 club. Doubled vulnerable, that's 500 points. The defense might do better (800), but no worse.

AN OPPONENT OVERCALLS 1NT

Suppose your partner opens the bidding with 1♡, the opponent bids 1NT and again you are the responder in 3rd chair.

1. ♠ A 7 5
   ♥ 7 6
   ♦ K Q J 9 3
   ♣ 10 9 7

2. ♠ K Q 10 8 7 5
   ♥ 6 5
   ♦ 8 7 6
   ♣ 9 3

3. ♠ K 7 6 5
   ♥ 9 7 4 3
   ♦ 7
   ♣ 10 5 4 2

1. With this hand stop and add. Your partner has about 13 points and you have 10. The NT bidder has about 17 and his partner is broke. 23 to 17. Double. They aren't going to make 1NT. Lead the K of diamonds. This time your suit is better than partner's. You have the ace of spades for an entry so you will typically get four diamond tricks. You should double for penalty with most hands of about 9 or more HCP. This is pretty universally played as penalty. A good way to get a lot of points. If for some rea-

son your 9 points don't work well for your side and the opponents happen to make the contract, they aren't doubled into game and you will not lose much.

2. Bid 2♠. Since you are expected to double with 9+ HCP, a new suit by you should be for play, showing typically a six-card suit and fewer than 9 HCP. A different way of looking at things. Notrump bids often change the meaning of subsequent bids.

3. Bid 2♡. The opponents most likely have more points than you, but with 4 hearts and a singleton, your hand will produce some tricks.

INTERFERENCE WITH THE UNUSUAL 2NT

Your partner opens 1♠ and the opponent bids 2NT, showing two long minors—typically played as two good minor suits of at least 5-5 and less than an opening hand. The idea by the opponents in making the two-suited preempt is an attempt to mess up your communication and make it difficult for you to get to the right game or maybe their side can make something if they fit well. Also, when your side is vulnerable and the opponents are not, sometimes they can make a cheap sacrifice at the five level when you were about to make four hearts or four spades.

As an aside, the reason 2NT is widely used as the unusual 2NT is because big NT hands can be shown by overcalling NT. Balanced hands that are bigger than 18 HCP can be shown by starting with a takeout double; and when partner has theoretically picked the trump suit, the doubler now bids NT. This is a much better way to show the bigger NT hand because sometimes a hand of about 20 points can be shown without leaving the one level as in the auction below.

East	South	West	North
1♢	Double	Pass	1♠
Pass	1NT		

Now, South has shown a balanced hand of about 20 points, and in this case is still at the one level. A real advantage when the North hand happens to be dreadful—a distinct possibility when West has opened and South has 20 points. That's about 33 points already used up.

As in a comparable situation in the last chapter, when the auction is crammed, the raise of partner's major suit should be more flexible, such as:

Partner   You
1♠   (2NT)   3♠

The 3♠ bid by you should be about 8-11 points including distribution (a good 2♠ bid). With a hand of opening strength you must bid game directly. You could cue-bid one of their suits, but that becomes a bit more involved when they have shown 2 suits. A straightforward treatment would be to bid 4♠ with an opening hand, and the only new suit left is the other major so a bid of 3♡ in this auction would show long hearts, 6 or more, and is a forcing bid so should be opening strength or the equivalent. 3NT would be for play. There are more sophisticated methods over these auctions, but they are somewhat involved and are easily forgotten because they come up infrequently. So until your partnership is highly evolved and your pride can handle the total loss of control when you have a mishap, simplicity is recommended. Yes, the auction is high and the bid gets in your way, but wait! There is a plus side.

Sometimes your have a pretty good hand, with length in one or both of their suits and shortness in partner's suit. Below are two sample hands after the auction 1♠ (2NT) by the opponents.

	1.		2.	
	♠	6 2	♠	8 2
	♥	A 7 6	♥	A J 9 2
	♦	K J 6 5	♦	A K 9 4 3
	♣	Q J 10 3	♣	6 5

With the first hand double now, and when the opponents settle on one of their minor suits, double that. Double with the second hand also. **The double shows that you are prepared to double at least one of their suits for penalty.** In the second hand you double and would love to see them land in a 3◊ contract, which you would happily double; and if they were to pick clubs, maybe partner has enough clubs to double that.

Chapter FIFTEEN
WHEN THE OPPONENTS COMPETE OVER OUR NOTRUMP OPENING BID

The opponents will sometimes interfere by bidding a long suit and some have ways of showing two-suited hands. Let's just start with an opponent who overcalled 2♡, showing a good six-card heart suit and probably a card or so outside. So the bidding has gone 1NT by your partner, 2♡ overcall, and you have the following hands:

1. ♠ A K 4 3   2. ♠ 6 4   3. ♠ A 5 2   4. ♠ 5 4
   ♥ 4 3   ♥ A J 9 2   ♥ 5 4   ♥ 6 5
   ♦ K 7 6 5   ♦ A 8 7   ♦ K Q J 5 4   ♦ 9 8 6
   ♣ 10 9 7   ♣ 10 9 8 5   ♣ 7 5 4   ♣ K Q J 6 5 4

Given that you have no special gimmicks to deal with each of these situations, see if you can come to a logical choice as to what your bid should be. No one is vulnerable.

The opponents sometimes have a reasonable bid and sometimes they are "out there," thinking they can mess up your Stayman auction.

1. Bid 3♡. Bidding their suit is Stayman. When they interfere at the 2 level 2♣ is no longer available to us and it doesn't follow that 3♣ is Stayman, although that might be a good guess. We want to use 3♣ for something else and 3♡ is an available bid that can be used for Stayman. In this case there is only one major suit left so opener bids 3♠, (4♠ with Maximum) or 3NT.
2. Double. You have four sure tricks defending 2♡, and partner with an opening notrump hand will produce three to four tricks if he becomes a defender. You normally get more points for doubling and it's almost surely a good score: 300-500 points, which is as good or better than your game, and a game for your side isn't even a certainty. Take the sure thing.
3. 3NT. Partner opened 1NT so a stopper by you is seldom needed. Partner is heavily favored to have a heart stopper or even two. His hand is better than yours and his points have to be somewhere.

4. Bid 3♣. We are well conditioned that new suits by responder are forcing, but notrump bidding is a different situation. You are the captain in notrump auctions, so if you wanted to be in 3NT you would already have done so. Your 3♣ bid is totally nonforcing—sort of a goodish drop-dead bid. The purpose of the bid is that with the 4th hand above, the opponents are very likely to make 2♡ as you have very little defense, maybe one trick. And—your club suit is good enough that your side is likely to make 3♣ opposite an opening notrump bid.

Notice in the last example (after a 1NT opening and a 2♡ overcall) a bid of 3♢ or 2♠ would be the same sort of thing—a goodish drop-dead bid. A 2♠ bid might look something like this

```
♠  K  10 8  7  5  4
♥  9
♦  6  5  4  3
♣  9  7
```

With only five spades the hand should be a bit better; a hand with which you expect to make 2♠.

Think about the meaning of a 3♠ bid. That is a jump, and should be 10+ points and five spades, trying to get to the best contract—4♠ or 3NT.

Notice that if the bidding were 1NT and 2♢ overcall, cue bidding 3♢ would be Stayman and would show at least one four-card major.

This is a rather uncomplicated method that works quite well. Some people play a variety of conventions after the interference, but most of the time the conventions are unnecessary and partnerships get them confused with such frequency that the straightforward approach listed will get you through most situations.

After you bid 1NT, if your LHO doubles, the standard meaning of the double is for penalty.

South (you)	West
1NT	Double

The double shows a balanced hand that is about 17 or more points, or it could be a long suit that will set up with entries to enjoy it, such as

♠ 8 5
♥ A 7 4
♦ K Q J 10 4 2
♣ A 3

With the K of ◇ lead on the above hand, West can count seven sure tricks. If his partner happens to have a winner, you will go down two tricks.

However, most of the time the person who doubles will have the big balanced hand, as big or bigger than the NT bidder. The reason is that if the NT bidder has 17 HCP and the next hand also has 17 points or *more,* the second hand has the strategic advantage because he is over the NT opener. The following is an example of 17 points in each of the first two hands and the remaining 6 points are divided evenly, 3 & 3. Look at the following hand:

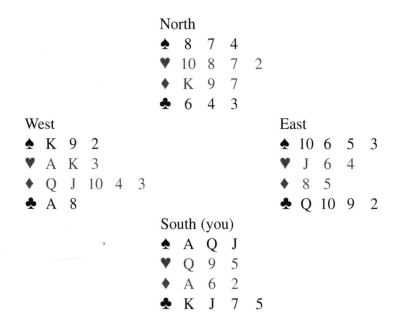

North
♠ 8 7 4
♥ 10 8 7 2
♦ K 9 7
♣ 6 4 3

West
♠ K 9 2
♥ A K 3
♦ Q J 10 4 3
♣ A 8

East
♠ 10 6 5 3
♥ J 6 4
♦ 8 5
♣ Q 10 9 2

South (you)
♠ A Q J
♥ Q 9 5
♦ A 6 2
♣ K J 7 5

In addition to West having 17 or more points it is important that he has a good opening lead. With this hand, West does have a good opening lead, the Q of diamonds. Although each side has 20 HCP, East/West has the advantage. You, as declarer, will be hard-pressed to come up with 7 tricks. You are very likely to go down more than one trick.

If your partner (North) has a little different sort of hand, one that is very weak such as 0 to 2 points, and he has a long suit, five or more cards, he should try to escape. With no special agreements or conventions, a bid of 2♣, 2◊, 2♡, & 2♠ would all be for play, a drop-dead bid, showing a 5-card suit or on a lucky day, a 6-card suit.

If he has five cards in any suit and a dreadful hand, the bid of 2 of a suit is likely to improve the contract. Even if you have only two cards in his suit, his bid is likely to improve the situation, because if you are in a 5-2 fit, his five-card suit is likely to take a couple of tricks when it is trump. If you happen to have three or four cards in the suit partner bids, he has struck oil. He may be able to make the contract.

Likewise, if the bidding goes 1NT (double) Pass, and back to you, if you happen to have a five-card suit you should bid it, unless of course, you think you can make 1NT. With a **five-card suit in either hand, 2 of a suit is likely to be a better contract.** Even if you go down, it is likely to be a smaller amount.

If North passes and East has a dreadful hand and a long suit, such as

♠ 9 8 6 5 3 2
♥ 5 4 2
♦ J
♣ 7 4 2

East will make no contribution to the defense, and North/South may have more than 20 points. His partner's double may not work out well and East is favored to make 2♠. He can get to his hand with trump and lead through the NT opener, and of course he will take several tricks in spades.

And what if East has this hand?   ♠ A 9 8 6 5 3 2
                                   ♥ — — —
                                   ♦ 10 9 8
                                   ♣ 7 5 4

He should have a good shot at making 4♠. If you were in his shoes, I trust you would bid it.

Chapter SIXTEEN
WHEN WE COMPETE WITH A
JUMP OVERCALL OR MICHAELS

There are numerous sorts of jump overcalls. We can make a jump over-call at the two level or three level. Some are a single jump (1♡ opening, 3♢ overcall), some a double jump (1♢ opening, 3♡ a double jump), or more (1♢ opening, 4♡ a big jump).

For the great majority of rubber bridge players, the single jump shows a strong hand—meaning too big to overcall. (The ceiling on an overcall of a suit is approximately 17 high.) Playing this style, (1♢, 2♠ a jump overcall) would be about 18-22 points, not forcing, but alerting partner to find a bid with a little something in his hand. Now comes the auction 1♡ opening, 3♢ overcall; and many times there is a bidding misunderstanding. If a single jump is played as strong, this auction is also a single jump and should be played the same. The confusion that has occurred for years and years in this auction is because logic dictates that it is strong, just like (1♢, 2♠), but when the bid is at the three level it sounds like a preempt—hence, confusion.

RECOMMENDATION - PLAY ALL JUMP OVERCALLS AS PREEMPTIVE.

This means that a jump overcall at the two level such as a 1♢ opening and a 2♠ overcall would also be weak. Before discussing how to show the stronger hand, let's clarify.

After a 1♣ bid by an opponent, these bids:
2♢, 3♡, 2♠, 3♠, 3♢, 4♢, 2♡, etc. would *ALL* be weak. This preemptive style has become so much accepted that many consider it to be standard. It is not the popularity of the jump overcall being treated as weak that influences me to recommend it; I recommend it because I think it is a good treatment. It is a good nuisance bid and there are other ways to show the very strong hand; plus the fact that the very strong hand doesn't occur often, and the preemptive jump overcall occurs fairly frequently, especially at the two level. With a bid that has two clear-cut ways it could be played, it is best to take nothing for granted. If you have a regular partner, discuss it and come to an agreement. The most important thing is that you and your partner have

the same agreement. That is more important than which way is best. If you are playing with someone and you have no idea how they would take it if you bid 2♠ after a 1◇ opener, try not to use the bid. Rather than invite trouble, bid 1♠, pass, or ask someone to fill in for you because you are going to make a phone call.

The difference between a preemptive jump overcall at the two level and three level is the number of cards: at the two level, six cards will do; and at the three level, seven cards. The preemptive bid at both levels shows a good suit, 2-3 honors, and less than an opening hand. Most of your values should be in your suit.

With no one vulnerable, after a 1♣ opening your 2♡ bid would look something like this:

> ♠ Q 4 2
> ♥ K Q J 7 5 4
> ♦ 4
> ♣ 10 9 4

The queen of spades could be a larger card, or your spades could be three small. It is the heart suit (and less than an opening hand) that beckons you to make a preemptive jump overcall.

On that rare occasion when you actually have a hand that is **too strong for an overcall,** about 18/19+ points, you will start out with a double.

Suppose the bidding is 1♣ on your right and you have

> ♠ 3 2
> ♥ A J 7 6 5 3
> ♦ A K Q 2
> ♣ A

You have 18 HCP plus a six-card heart suit. Start out with a double. If partner bids 1♠ you will next bid 2♡ which should be a wake-up call to partner. You ask him to pick the trump suit and then you dismiss his bid and bid 2♡. This shows a hand that is too good to overcall 1♡. You have a legitimate fear that partner would pass an overcall but has just enough for you to make a game, such as with the following hand:

Partner's hand   ♠   Q   7   5   4
                     ♥   K   8
                     ♦   9   8   7   5
                     ♣   9   8   2

You most often have six hearts when you double and change suits, and partner has enough that he should make some sort of a sound—3♥ would be good, and you will get to a nice spot of 4♥.

> WHEN YOU MAKE A TAKEOUT DOUBLE AND OVER
> PARTNER'S BID YOU CHANGE TO A NEW SUIT OR
> NOTRUMP, YOU ARE SHOWING A VERY BIG HAND.

MICHAELS CUE BID

The most common use of the Michaels cue bid is over an opponent's 1♣ or 1◇ opening. The second hand bids the opponent's suit, 2♣ or 2 ◇. If playing Michaels, these bids would show 5-5 or more in the majors—the major suits are good, but the hand is less than opening strength. Some also use it over the major openings showing the other major and an undisclosed minor suit. To find out what the minor suit is, you would have to bid 2NT, and partner would then name his minor suit. In any of the hands in this book, the samples will be just over minor-suit openings. This is the best way to start playing Michaels, (and probably the best way, period) as it occurs more often, keeps the bidding lower; and it is safer. Over minor-suit openings, Michaels is a very effective constructive bid, not primarily an interference bid. It very often allows you to find a part score and even a game with less than the usual points.

Having one bid to show two suits can be very effective. South opens 1♣ and you are West and bid 2♣ with the following hand

                           ♠   K   Q   6   5   4
                           ♥   K   J   10 7   5
                           ♦   6   5
                           ♣   9

If the bulk of the points belong to the opponents, your bid often makes it more difficult for them to proceed—the one level is used up for one thing.

Another situation could be that the person in third chair may want to bid 3NT but has stoppers in only one of your two five-card majors.

For your information, after the 2♣ or 2◇ bid responder can bid 2♡ to suggest that he has hearts stopped and is thinking of notrump. The opener, with any sort of balanced hand and spades stopped, should bid notrump. If he bids 2NT, responder can now take it to 3NT; much more fuss and possible misunderstandings for the opponents than if they had the one level available and could bid their hands normally.

Back to the bidding for your side. Suppose the auction is as follows:

West (You)	North	East	South
			1♣
2♣	Pass	?	

Your partner can have a good-fitting hand or one that doesn't fit well.

		Your hand again
1. ♠ 3	2. ♠ A 8 7 2	♠ K Q 6 5 4
♥ Q 2	♥ 3	♥ K J 10 7 5
◆ K J 8 7 2	◆ A 8 7 4	◆ 6 5
♣ K 8 7 4 3	♣ A 8 5 4	♣ 9

The first hand appears to be a problem for your partner. He should not even *think* of passing 2♣; he should calmly bid 2♡. Although this might not be a great contract, the next opponent may bid and partner is off the hook. Only if 2♡ is doubled will this probably be a poor score for you and that doesn't happen often. If 2♡ is not doubled there is no problem.

Now look at the second hand. This hand is filled with so many positive things going for it: a fourth trump—meaning nine between you—a singleton, and two aces to cover 2 of the 3 minor-suit losers partner has. 4♠ is the winning call! A nice game contract with only 21 HCP. In fact, you are favored to make five. You would probably make four with one of the minor suit aces removed from the hand.

Chapter SEVENTEEN
LIMIT RAISES MADE SIMPLE

For years tournament players have been playing that a bid of 1♡ or 1♠ followed by a jump in that suit by responder is invitational rather than forcing. The jump, such as

Auction #1 Opener	Opponent	Responder
1♠	(Pass)	3♠

shows 10+ to a 12- points. This bid is called a limit raise. As stated, this bid is fairly standard in competitive bridge circles, but the great majority of bridge players in this country play social or rubber bridge, not tournament bridge. Most of the social or rubber bridge players play the above jump raise as an opening hand.

There are some advantages in playing limit raises. A suggestion regarding whether or not to play limit raises is the "when in Rome" theory. If all the players in your social group or groups play the bid as forcing, and you play with a variety of partners, play it their way. If you feel compelled to ask, rather than using the term limit raises, ask what it would mean if "my partner opens 1♡ and I bid 3♡."

However, if you have one or two partners that you play with almost all of the time, the two of you can decide whether you want to play limit or forcing raises in a major suit.

The limit raise replaces the temporizing auction:

Auction #2.	South	West	North	East
	1♠	Pass	2♣	Pass
	2NT	Pass	3♠	

The above is an example of how people who play *forcing* major-suit raises would bid the hand that is just a little too good for 1♠—2♠ (6 to 10), but not good enough for 1♠—3♠ (13+). The auction #2 is an example that shows the point range of 10+ to 12-.

Playing limit raises the responder can show this hand in one quick bid with a jump to 3♠. One big advantage to the limit raise is that it is much more difficult for the opponents to overcall. In auction #2, after the 2♣ bid, East can overcall 2◇ or 2♡. Over a 3♠ limit bid, he is highly unlikely to come bounding in at the four level, such as with 4♡.

Suppose your suit is hearts and you and partner bid 1♡—3♡; again a 3♠ overcall is very unlikely to occur. If East has the opportunity to overcall 2♠ there are many more hands which would qualify for a two-level overcall than a three-level overcall. Hence, the 3♡ bid often blocks out the opponents. Some hands can make 3♡ in one direction and 3♠ in the other. They will seldom be able to discover their spade fit when you bid 3♡.

Your partner opens 1♡ and you have
♠ A 2
♥ 9 8 4 3
♦ A J 6 2
♣ 10 9 5

9 HCP, a doubleton, and a 4th trump (meaning 9 trump together) for about 11 points. This is a classic limit raise.

Many who play limit raises require four-card trump support by responder. Although there is some value in this, it is more complicated and the objective in this chapter is to keep it simple. You and your partner have agreed to play limit raises and your partner opens 1♡. Look at the next three hands:

1. ♠ 3 2
   ♥ A 8 7
   ♦ Q 4 3 2
   ♣ Q J 8 4

2. ♠ 9 5 2
   ♥ A 8 7
   ♦ A Q 10 5
   ♣ 10 8 4

3. ♠ 3 2
   ♥ K 4 3 2
   ♦ A Q 10 2
   ♣ 6 4 3

1. Bid 2♡. Don't get carried away. This is a 10 count without a hint of gold. The diamond queen will often be useless because there are no good cards with it. This hand has 10 bad points, not 10 good.
2. 3♡. You have only three hearts, but your hand is a very good 10 because of the good diamond suit and 2 aces.
3. 3♡. 10 golden points—11 actually, counting a point for the 4th trump.

So now what do you do with other types of hands with heart support?

1. ♠ 3		2. ♠ 4 3	
♥ K 8 6 3 2		♥ A Q 4 3	
♦ Q J 10 3		♦ 8 6	
♣ 6 4 3		♣ A J 9 3 2	

1. Bid 4♡. You don't want to play anything that deprives you of making a 4♡ bid with this "magic hand." It is a tremendous blocking bid if the 4th person has a good hand. Playing limit raises shouldn't affect this bid. The jump by responder to 4♡ is played the same as it has been forever.
2. Now you have an opening hand with heart support. With this hand bid 2♣, and when partner rebids 2◇, 3♣, 2NT or similar, *jump* to 4♡.

There are several other ways to show the opening hand with support for partner's major, but this treatment is easy and works just fine.

It is possible to play limit raises in the minor suits, but there are several problems that occur, so it may be best to play limit raises only in the major suits and leave jumps in the minor suits as forcing. This is a simple but a good practical way to play limit raises.

We have a much more detailed discussion in *Major Suit Raises: Many Kinds, Many Choices*. See a list of the BRIDGE Mini Series in the back of this book.

Chapter EIGHTEEN
INTRODUCTION TO
WEAK TWO-BIDS

Opening the bidding with two of a suit has been a strong, forcing-to-game bid for many years. The trend has been moving more and more to opening bids of 2◇, 2♡, and 2♠ as weak two-bids. The weak two-bid is a hand of about 6-10 HCP with a good six-card suit.

Until recent years, mostly tournament players used weak two-bids. The bids of 2◇, 2♡, and 2♠, as weak two-bids have been growing so much in popularity that many social or rubber bridge players also are using them. Some bridge teachers use them from the get go while others like starting out with the more traditional strong twos and eventually switching over. My preference is the latter because weak twos require more judgment, and in the early stages of learning, I prefer to avoid the artificial 2♣ bid and the complexities that go with it.

- HOWEVER, teachers and players should use what works best for them, and also be willing to adapt to what is being used in their area.

In any case, you may want to have a working knowledge of both, because you will want to play what is being used in your area or by your group, and be prepared when invited to play with a new group. You will want to understand the bidding of those with whom you play, as well as be understood. Bridge is a game of communication and not about which person is right. With the belief that weak twos are more and more the direction in which we are moving, here is the scoop.

The following hands qualify for an opening bid of 2♠:

	♠ A Q J 7 5 2	or	♠ A Q 10 8 6 2
	♥ 6 4 3		♥ K 5 4
	◆ 2		◆ 2
	♣ 9 8 6		♣ 9 7 4

The requirments for opening with a weak two-bid:

- A good six-card suit—two or three honors.
- 6-10 HCP
- An outside honor may or may not be in the hand.
- Vulnerability is a factor. When you are vulnerable the suit should be quite good: No one vulnerable is an average situation, and you might be a bit frisky if the opponents are vulnerable and you are not.

The bid is effective for a couple of very good reasons: One is if the opponents happen to have the bulk of the points (or think they do) they will have trouble communicating when the bidding is so high before they get a chance to speak. Often, they will overbid, underbid, or land in the wrong suit. The other reason the bid works well is that after your partner opens a weak two-bid, you should have a pretty good idea what to do, as his bid is quite descriptive.

Suppose your partner opens the bidding with 2♠ and you have the following hand:

Your hand	♠ K 9 3
	♥ A 9 8 7
	♦ K Q 3
	♣ J 10 4

Partner's hands	1. ♠ A Q J 7 5 2	2. ♠ A Q 10 8 6 2
	♥ 6 4 3	♥ K 5 4
	♦ 2	♦ 2
	♣ 8 5 4	♣ 9 7 4

Your K93 is good spade support (nine of them between you), 13 solid points, and a good supply of quick tricks. But, if you glance at your losers with your hand opposite the partner's first hand, you will see none in spades, two in hearts, one in diamonds, and three in clubs. That means that 2♠ may go down. If diamonds are played before hearts, you can shed a heart or two so 2♠ may well make, but 4♠ has no chance.

Opposite hand #2, although partner is at the top of his bid for a weak two-bid, you have no spade losers, one heart loser, one diamond loser and three club losers. The diamond suit should absorb your heart loser.

Nonetheless, you have three club losers and the ace of diamonds that can be taken before you ever get the lead.

You have a good hand. What is wrong with this picture? It is quite simple really: Partner has less than an opening hand so you will need more than an opening hand to even think of bidding a game. With a balanced 13 count, don't even think about bidding 4♠. With the exception of a highly distributional hand that fits well, you need more than a balanced 13, and usually 14 will not be enough to have a shot at game.

For you to bid 4♠ without any questions of partner, your hand should look something like one of the hands below:

♠ 9 4	♠ K 9 3	♠ K 4 3
♥ A Q 7	♥ A Q J	♥ 7
♦ A 8 6 3	♦ Q 6 4	♦ K 7 5 4
♣ A K 3 2	♣ A Q 5 2	♣ A K 10 3 2

With all of these hands partner should either be able to make 4♠ or at least have a good chance at making the contract. The third hand has good perks.

With a borderline hand (about 15 or 16 playing points), 2NT is used for further inquiry about partner's opening two-bid. The information will help you decide if you have enough to bid a game (occasionally a slam).

With the hand below, you are good enough to ask for more information after partner opens with 2♠.

Your hand

North
♠ K 8
♥ Q J 10
♦ Q 10 6 3
♣ A K 5 4

♠ A Q J 7 5 2   Partner's second hand
♥ K 4 3   listed again for your
♦ 2   convenience.
♣ 9 8 6

Bid 2NT with the north hand. You are asking partner if, in addition to a good spade suit, he has an outside honor card (a feature) in the hand. The 2NT bid by you asks partner to name that feature. He will do so by bidding 3♡, which you know is the A or K (you have the Q and J). You also know that he is almost certainly not holding a very minimum hand for his weak two-bid because he has a good suit and a feature. The feature, along with two or more honors in his suit, usually brings his point count to 8-10, rather than 6-7. Partner's 3♡ bid is good news: The heart honor fits well with your Q, J, and 10. After you hear 3♡, you bid 4 ♠.

Some people show a feature with QJ2 of the suit, which is okay, but the most common treatment is that a feature is an A or K. If partner has no feature, he will simply rebid his suit. If he does have a feature, you will know which suit contains the feature, because partner bids it when you ask with 2NT. If the feature fits with your hand, because it is in a suit in which you also have an honor or honors, you obviously have a good fit. If partner were to show a feature in a situation where you had three little cards, or a singleton, the feature is less valuable to you.

With the following hands, which hands qualify for a weak two-bid?

1. ♠ A K
   ♥ J 9 8 7 5 3
   ♦ Q 6 5
   ♣ 9 2

2. ♠ K J 10 7 6 5
   ♥ A 5 4
   ♦ 5 3
   ♣ 9 7

3. ♠ 4 3
   ♥ A K 7 6 5 4
   ♦ 8 6
   ♣ 10 9 3

4. ♠ 5 4
   ♥ A 3
   ♦ 9 8 5
   ♣ A J 10 9 6 5

1. No, you have a lousy suit. (You need two, or better yet, three honors.)
2. Open with 2♠.
3. Open with 2♡.
4. No, no, no. 2♣ is saved for very big hands.

After partner opens a weak two-bid:
1. Pass with little fit and an opening hand.
2. Bid 2NT (to ask for feature) with **invitational** hands.
3. Raise partner's suit from two to three. The raise is further preemptive, **not an invitation.** Notice this is a new way of thinking. Partner opens 2♡ and

you bid 3♡. In other types of auctions raises are invitational, but the meaning is different here so partner should **never** bid 4♡ after your raise to 3♡.

4. Bid game if your hand qualifies, i.e., 2♡—4♡

5. Bid a new suit with five or **six+** cards with a strong hand, well above opening strength, when you are interested in game but don't know which one to bid (2◊—2♡). Partner should raise you with any three cards, honor doubleton (Q3) and consider it with two small. If partner has no support at all, he rebids his suit. After a weak two-bid, a new suit by responder is forcing.

The 2♣ opening bid

The 2♣ opening bid is reserved for all very big hands.

With a hand such as:

1.	♠	A K J 7 5 2	or	2.	♠	A Q J 7 5
	♥	A K Q 5			♥	A Q J 8 6
	♦	9			♦	A K Q
	♣	A Q			♣	— — —

those who are playing strong two bids open 2♠, while those playing weak twos open 2♣, wait for partner's expected 2◊ bid, and now they show their suit by bidding 2♠. A recommendation at this point in your bidding is to play that your 2♠ bid is forcing to game.

With the 2nd hand above, you will open with 2♣ and if partner bids 2◊, you will bid 2♠. If your suit is not raised, you will want to bid your hearts at least once and possibly twice to show your two five-card suits. It is reassuring to know that partner will keep making verbal sounds with the purpose of helping you pick the trump suit for game (occasionally slam).

The 2◊ response by partner is referred to as a waiting bid, or another term which is very descriptive, "semi-automatic" (almost automatic), for indeed, partner will bid 2◊ with all hands except when he has a good five-card suit or longer—typically 2 of the top 3 honors or better in the suit, AK972, for example.

Therefore, the 2◇ bid says nothing about size; just denies a strong five-card suit.

A hand to practice bidding:

South	North
♠ A J 2	♠ K Q 10 5 4
♥ K Q J 6 4	♥ 7 3
♦ A K Q J	♦ 9 3 2
♣ 8	♣ A 7 6

South (you)	North
2♣	2♠
4NT	5◇
6♠	

Another hand to practice bidding:

♠ A K J 3 2   Partner's hand not shown
♥ A 6 5
♦ K Q J 2
♣ A

South (you)	North
2♣	2◇
2♠	3♡
4♡	

Partner has denied a strong five-card heart suit (or longer) when he didn't bid 2♡ right away. The delayed heart bid suggests he has length, but lacks strength in the suit, so slam looks unlikely. If partner's heart suit is something like K98732 (six of them) and he has an outside A, he can still try for slam after you bid 4♡.

Having the 2♣ bid as artificial, you can rebid notrump to show big balanced hands. A good treatment to strong balanced hands is as follows:

2NT opening	=	21-22 HCP
2♣—2◇—2NT	=	23-24 HCP
3NT opening	=	25-26 HCP
2♣—2◇—3NT	=	27-28 HCP

The above chart is another benefit of the weak two-bid structure. With the artificial 2♣ opening, you have the opportunity to show more sizes and very specific ranges of strong balanced hands.

Chapter NINETEEN
THE EVOLUTION OF
HAND EVALUATION

It is intriguing to look over the years of hand evaluation and the ever-changing approaches. In 1913 Milton Work wrote his first book on auction bridge and from 1917 for over a decade he was considered to be the leading authority on bridge. In his book, Auction Methods, written in 1920, his minimum-opening bid of one of a suit was

♠ x x
♥ A K x x x
♦ x x x
♣ x x x

which was an estimated four tricks in the heart suit. The suit didn't have to be a major. He, along with Whitehead, another known writer and a top player, described a notrump opening as three suits safely stopped, such as the following hand taken from Work's book:

♠ A K x
♥ J 10 x x
♦ K J x x
♣ x x

It wasn't that people were less clever; but rather, that there are no absolutes as to what these definitions should be, and bridge has evolved tremendously.

Along came Josephine and Ely. These were household names starting in the mid '20s. The Culbertsons were stars. They were the top-ranking husband and wife pair in the nation, wrote columns, books, and taught bridge. With the country consumed with bridge, people were playing in trains, bus stops, on lunch hours, anywhere they could—bridge had hit the country like a storm. The Culbertsons grew rich with their book sales, columns, and Ely was making $10,000 a week on just a radio contract alone. He was colorful, flamboyant, and spent money extravagantly. So while the nation was facing the great depression, people continued to play bridge; it was an inexpensive hobby, and Ely, their fearless leader, who was considered to be the best player in the country, was rolling in riches.

Their popularity was enhanced because they wrote bridge books that were understandable and had a broad appeal. Although their style seems archaic now, the Culbertsons added a bit of sophistication to bidding of that day. Some of the bidding practices attributed to them were:

A minimum opening contained $2^1/_2$ to 3 honor tricks—$2^1/_2$ if there was a good five-card suit, and 3 honor tricks if there was only a four-card suit or a weak five-card suit. Honor tricks were estimated winners with high cards.

An opening bid of 1NT was exactly 4-3-3-3 distribution and exactly $3^1/_2$ or 4 honor tricks. Josephine cautioned against bidding notrump too freely, but said regarding a 1NT opener—"when correctly used (it) is a very beautiful bid."

Culbertson was the first person of authority to treat short suits (doubletons, singletons, and voids) as valuable and sometimes even more valuable than high cards. He was also the first well-known person to introduce the idea that new suits are forcing. (It's hard to imagine playing bridge without the assumption that a new suit by responder is forcing.) In 1938 Ely became consumed with WWII in Europe so was not playing much bridge.

So, in the late '40s enters Goren. He also was very prolific and, as many of you know, introduced the world to point-count bidding. It wasn't as if the idea hadn't occurred to others of his day, but they chose to use honor tricks as their main criterion for opening the bidding. With point-count bidding, people found hand evaluation a much easier task. Goren's method was quite simple: Count your HCP and add distribution points for short suits right from the beginning.

For quite a number of years Goren ruled the bridge world. Then, as always seems to be the case in bridge, little changes began to creep in until the bidding was no longer very much like what he originally wrote. To list a few of those changes:

■ Five-card majors became very popular and spread like wildfire, even though Goren's writing was still opening four-card majors. This change did not come without a battle. At teachers' conferences this was a most unsettling debate. When people had been teaching a certain way for a long period of time and their materials were all made up accordingly, this was no small matter. Five-card major suit openings affected a number of other things as well, such as the responder's raises. But there was no stopping the popularity of five-card majors. From then on bridge theorists as well as any bridge player with a pencil and paper began contributing their ideas.

- Some added a point(s) for long suits if the suit contained 6 or 7 HCP.
- Some quit counting short suit points until a trump suit was found.
- Some began opening all hands with 12 HCP.
- Some began counting a point for any five-card suit.
- Some began to evaluate a hand in terms of a fairly complicated method of loser count after the trump suit had been picked (this had been used before Goren's writing and resurfaced again later).
- Some began counting HCP and counting the number of cards in the two longest suits, and they would open if the total came to 20 or more.
- And in the words of the King, "Et cetera, et cetera, et cetera."

Somewhere along the line there became little resemblance to what Goren wrote. Although bidding now is considerably different than what it was, Goren should be given considerable credit. The game of bridge would not be where it is today had it not been for him.

So what is the best method of hand evaluation? As you can see, the methods of hand evaluation have been in constant motion since bridge first became popular. I see no reason to think it will ever stop changing. Interestingly enough, of the many methods of hand evaluation that are around today, they all come out fairly evenly, from Goren up to the one that was just thought up yesterday. **It is an indication of how fascinated people are with bridge.** As to which method is best, Oswald Jacoby probably nailed it down when he said, "The best one hasn't been invented yet."

Is this cause for confusion? No, not unless you choose to let it be so. Read about some of the different ideas and use what works best for you, which may end up being a blend of some of the different thoughts. Normally, the only time it matters is when you have a decision to make and you are on the cusp. Using your judgment, which is ultimately what you need to do, takes time; and if you consider yourself a student of the game, you will keep learning as long as you play.

As a teacher as well as a student of the game, I often get asked about how long it takes to learn bridge. I tell them, "For the rest of your life." Also, having been involved with music all of my life, I might add, "It's kind of like learning to play the piano. It depends on if you want to play 'Yankee Doodle' or Rachmaninov."

SCORING

Bidding starts with the number of tricks you hope to take over six. A bid of three is contracting for nine tricks.

For contracts bid and made the score is: Minor suits = 20 points per trick

    Major suits = 30 points per trick

    No Trump = 40 points for the first trick, 30 for each subsequent trick

GAME IS 100 POINTS OR MORE

WE	THEY

Game bids vary depending on where the contract is played:

5♣ or 5◇ (11 tricks) is game as 5 x 20 = 100 points

4♡ or 4♠ (10 tricks) is game as 4 x 30 = 120 points

3NT (9 tricks) is game as 40 + 30 + 30 = 100 points

The points recorded below the line record the contracts which are bid and made. There are various bonuses that can be made—they are recorded above the line.

Whichever side wins two games first wins what's known as a "rubber." The advantage of winning a rubber is that you receive 500 or 700 bonus points for this, 500 if the opponents have scored one game and 700 points if they have not.

Game can be scored all in one hand or part at a time. If on one hand you bid 3◇ and make three, you have 60 points (below the line). If on a later hand you bid 2♠ and take the eight tricks necessary, you score 60 more points below the line. 60 + 60 is greater than 100, so you have scored a game. part at a time. If, however, the opponents make a game after your 3◇ bid, but before your 2♠ bid, your partial no longer counts towards your game.

A SAMPLE RUBBER

1. N/S bid 2♡ made 3.

2. E/W bid 3NT, made 3.
   E/W vulnerable.

3. N/S bid 1 NT, made 1.

4. N/S bid 3♣, made 4.
   N/S vulnerable.*

5. E/W bid 4♠, made 4.

6. Bonus points for
   winning rubber.

	North/South WE		East/West THEY	
	4.	20		
	1.	30	500	6.
	1.	60	100	2.
	3.	40		
	4.	60		
			120	5.
		210	720	

E/W won by 510 points

Vulnerable means that you have won a game and are now in position to win the rubber if you win another game.

In the previous example, no one failed to make his bid. If one side fails to make their bid, the other side gets penalty points above the line. If the side that fails to make their contract has no game scored in the current rubber, they lose 50 points for each trick that they are short. If they are vulnerable (a game scored) they lose 100 points for each short trick.

50 POINTS FOR EACH TRICK SHORT, NON-VULNERABLE

100 POINTS FOR EACH TRICK SHORT, VULNERABLE

A SAMPLE SCORE

WE		THEY	
		50	4.
3.	200	50	1.
		100	2.

1. N S bid 4♠ and took only nine tricks. Notice they got no credit for the tricks they took, since it was less than what they bid.
2. EW bid and made 5◇.
3. E W bid 5♣ and took only nine tricks.
4. N S bid 3♡ and took only eight tricks. Notice it's still only 50 points as N S still isn't vulnerable.

If a contract is doubled, meaning the opponents feel they can defeat the contract, the score is:

NON-VULNERABLE	VULNERABLE
100 for the 1st trick short	200 for the 1st trick short
200 for the next two tricks	300 for each one thereafter
300* for each trick starting at 4 or more	

If, however, a person does make a doubled contract, they get their trick scores doubled (2♡ doubled making would be 60 x 2 = 120 for tricks) plus 50 points above the line for the "insult". When the doubled trick score totals over 100, as in the case of 2♡ doubled, credit is also given for the game, even though it wasn't bid.

If a doubled contract is redoubled, the trick scores are doubled again; 1♡ doubled and redoubled is 120. The overtricks or undertricks count twice as much as doubled contracts. The insult is 100 points if a redoubled contract is made.

OTHER BONUS POINTS
SMALL SLAM	500 points non-vulnerable
GRAND SLAM	1000 points non-vulnerable
SMALL SLAM	750 points vulnerable
GRAND SLAM	1500 points vulnerable

HOLDING 4 HONORS OF A SUIT YOU NAME AS TRUMP	100 PTS
HOLDING 5 HONORS OF A SUIT YOU NAME AS TRUMP	150 PTS
HOLDING ALL 4 ACES IN A NO TRUMP CONTRACT	150 PTS

*The revised scoring method now used for doubled-nonvulnerable contracts, i.e., 100, 300, 500, 800, 1100, etc.

CONTRACT		OUT
WE	THEY	SCORE
1		
2		
3		
4		
5		
6		
7		
8		
9		
10		
11		
12		
SUBTOTAL		
13		
14		
15		
16		
17		
18		
19		
20		
21		
22		
23		
24		
SUBTOTAL		
25		
26		
27		
28		
29		
30		
31		
32		
33		
34		
35		
36		
SUBTOTAL		
GRAND TOTAL		

NAME:

**NORMA SANDS
RECOMMENDED
QUICK SCORE**

EVERYTHING
SCORED IS
NONVULNERABLE

PART SCORE
Add trick scores plus
50 bonus for partscore.

GAME
Add trick scores plus
300 bonus for game.

SMALL SLAM
Add trick scores and
two bonuses:
300 (for game)
500 Small Slam bonus.

GRAND SLAM
Add trick scores and
two bonuses:
300 (for game)
1000 for Grand Slam bonus.

FAILED CONTRACTS
The opponenets get 50 for
each trick you go down.

NO CREDIT FOR
HONORS

This page may be repro-
duced. Copyright 2002.
Rocky Mountain Books

Scoring Examples

1. You bid 2♠ and took 8 tricks.
   Trick scores: 2 x 30 = 60
                                  +   <u>50</u>   part-score bonus
                                  110 **total points**

   If you made four, the score would be 60 more for 170 (you took 10 tricks, but did not bid the game, so the part-score bonus applies.)

2. You bid 3NT and took 9 tricks.
   Trick scores: 40 + 30 + 30 = 100
                                    + <u>300</u>   game bonus
                                    400 **total points**

3. You bid 6♡ and made 6 (12 tricks).
   Trick scores: 6 x 30 = 180
                                  + 300   game bonus
                                  + <u>500</u>   Small Slam bonus
                                  980 **total points**

   If you took all 13 tricks, the score would be 1010.

4. You're having a good day. You bid 7♠ and took all of the tricks.
   Trick scores: 7 x 30 = 210
                                  +   300   game bonus
                                  + <u>1000</u>   Grand Slam bonus
                                 1510 **total points**

Defeated contracts are the same as always when nonvulnerable:
50 points to the opponents for each trick you are short.

Doubled
100 / Down 1
300 / Down 2
500 / Down 3
800* / Down 4

* Scoring change now being used: Down four or more, each trick equals 300 points. Hopefully you won't have to calculate this one unless it's in your favor.

GLOSSARY

AUCTION   the bidding.

BLACKWOOD   a conventional bid of 4NT which asks partner how many aces he has.

BOOK   the first six tricks taken by the declarer.

CONTRACT   the final bid-(a double and redouble would be included as a part of the contract).

CONVENTION   an artificial bid which, by partnership agreement, asks a question or describes a particular type of hand, other than what is suggested by the bid itself.

DECLARER   the person within the partnership who first bid the suit (or NT) selected   as the final contract. This person plays both his hand and the dummy.

DEFEATED   The way you feel when you lose.

DISTRIBUTIONAL POINTS   points given in the evaluation of a hand for doubletons, singletons, or voids, also for extra length.

DOUBLE   a call made during the bidding which will increase the penalty points if the opponents fail to make their contract.

DOUBLETON   a suit containing only two cards.

DUMMY   the hand opposite declarer which is spread faceup on the table during the play of the hand.

FINESSE   an attempt to win a trick with a lower card when there is a higher card outstanding. (see sample hand at the end of Chapter 2).

FORCING BID   a bid that partner should not pass at his next turn.

GAME   scoring 100 points or more below the line. It can be accomplished part at a time (more than one hand) if the opponents don't bid a game in between.

HIGH CARD POINTS (HCP)   the value of a hand in terms of its high cards, A,K,Q,J.

HONORS   The A,K,Q,J,10 of a suit. In scoring, the points received for any one hand holding four or five of them in the trump suit or all four aces if the contracts is NT.

JUMP SHIFT   a deliberate one-level jump to a new suit by responder or opener, for example, 1♡—2♠ or 1◇—1♡—2♠.

LHO   left-hand opponent

LIMIT RAISE   A jump in partner suit (i.e., 1♡-3♡) showing invitational values about 11 or so points.

MAJOR SUITS   hearts and spades.

MINOR SUITS   clubs and diamonds.

NOTRUMP   a contract without a trump suit or a bid suggesting play without a trump suit.

NONVULNERABLE   the state of a pair which has not made a game in the current rubber.

ONE-OVER-ONE BID   a bid of a new suit on the one level after partner has opened the bidding with one of a suit.

OVERTRICKS   extra tricks taken after the contract has been fulfilled.

OVERCALLS   a bid of a suit or NT after an opponent has opened the auction.

PARTIAL or PART SCORE   bidding and making of a contract for which the score is less than 100 points.

PREEMPTIVE BID   a high-level bid which is intended to interfere with the opponents auction by taking their bidding space. It is made with long suits and weak hands.

PREEMPTIVE JUMP OVERCALLS   a treatment that defines your jump overcalls at the two or three level as weak.

QUICK TRICKS   high honors in a suit which are expected to win the first or second time the suit is led.

REBID   1. opener's rebid is his second bid.
            2. to bid your suit twice.

REDOUBLE   a bid which increases again either the score for making the doubled contract or the penalty for failure to do so.

REVERSE   a second bid on the two level or higher in a suit which is higher ranking than the first suit bid (1♢—1 ♠—2♡).

RHO   right-hand opponent.

RUBBER   two-game contracts made by one side.

RUFF   to play a trump when unable to follow suit.

RULE OF 2 OR 3   the number of tricks that a person may be willing to go down when they preempt—vulnerable or nonvulnerable.

SEQUENCE   three or more touching cards of which the highest is an honor.

SET   to defeat a contract.

SINGLETON   a suit containing only one card.

SLAM   a bid of six or seven.

SLUFF   to discard when out of the suit led.

STAYMAN   a conventional bid of 2♣ after partner has opened 1NT. The bid is intended to ask opener if his hand contains a four-card major.

SUIT RANK   the order in which suits must be bid on the same level. The rank beginning with the lowest is clubs, diamonds, hearts, and spades. Notrump is higher-ranking than any suit.

TAKEOUT DOUBLE   a double which is intended as a request for partner to bid.

TRICK   the four cards resulting after a card has been played from each hand. The highest card of the suit led wins the trick, unless it has been trumped.

TRUMP   a suit named as the master suit in the auction.

TWO-OVER-ONE-BID   responding on the two level with a new suit which is lower-ranking than the one partner opened, for example 1♡—2♣.

VOID   holding no cards of a suit.

VULNERABLE   the state of a pair which has made one game in the current rubber.

WEAK TWO BIDS   an opening bid of 2◇, 2♡, or 2♠ showing a preemptive sort of hand—typically a good six-card suit and about 6-10 HCP.

BRIDGE Mini Series
Awarded the 1992
Bridge Book of the Year

THE BRIDGE Mini Series

by Norma Sands & (Mr.) Jan Janitschke

I   Fine Tuning Your Bridge
Minor suit openings, help suit game tries and judgment situations.

II   Later in the Auction
Responses's 2nd turn, opener's 3rd turn reverses, bidding after a 2 over 1 bid.

III   Opening Leads Versus Suits
Analyzing the auction, leads to avoid, aggressive and passive leads.

IV   Double Trouble
Takeout, penalty, lead-directing doubles, and redoubles.

V   Weak Two Bids
Opening with a weak two bid responses, 2♣ bid, games and slams.

VI   Competitive Bidding
Overcalls at the one and two level, unusual NT, Michaels.

VII   Defensive Signals
Attitude signals, leads, count signals, suit preference signals.

VIII   Negative Doubles
After various level overcalls, related sequences.

IX   Slam Bidding I
Suit slams, quizzes, cue bidding and splinters.

X   Slam Bidding 11
NT slams, 4NT Blackwood or quantitative?
Gerber, how aggressive to be.

Each Mini Series $3.95 plus $3.00 and handling—one time charge, not per item. Send check or money order to Rocky Mountain Books. No need to call unless you are a teacher and want quantity orders.

More Mini Series Coming in 2002

Major Suit Raises Many Kinds Many Choices
When We Compete in Their NT Auction
Jocoby Transfers and Four-Suit Transfers

Rocky Mountain Books
P.O. Box 100663
Denver, CO 80210
see website www.normasands.com